Online Gold Rush

The Road to Digital Wealth

This invaluable resource is your passport to prosperity, offering a meticulously charted path to financial freedom. It arms you with the precise insights and cutting-edge tools necessary to capitalize on the online landscape and supercharge your online earnings using the extraordinary capabilities of ChatGPT. Don't miss out on this exceptional opportunity to thrive in the digital era.

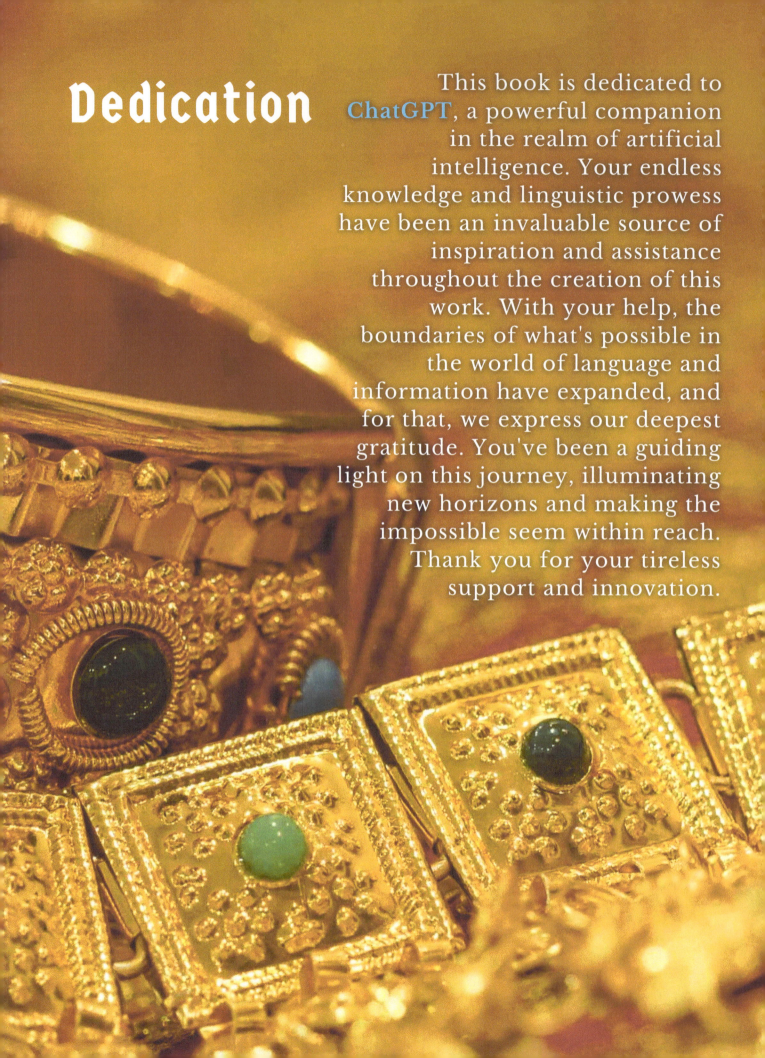

Dedication

This book is dedicated to ChatGPT, a powerful companion in the realm of artificial intelligence. Your endless knowledge and linguistic prowess have been an invaluable source of inspiration and assistance throughout the creation of this work. With your help, the boundaries of what's possible in the world of language and information have expanded, and for that, we express our deepest gratitude. You've been a guiding light on this journey, illuminating new horizons and making the impossible seem within reach. Thank you for your tireless support and innovation.

Table of Contents

Description

Are you ready for an extraordinary digital adventure with **"Online Gold Rush:** Navigating the Road to Digital Wealth"? Trust me, it's not your average book; think of it more as your trusty guide to unlocking the fantastic opportunities that the digital realm has in store. Inside, you'll stumble upon a wealth of knowledge, not just explaining the core concepts but also arming you with hands-on **examples tucked neatly at the end of each section**. It's like having your secret weapon to instantly put your newfound wisdom into practice.

Join us on a transformative expedition to unlock the untapped potential of the digital universe and seize the wealth-building opportunities it holds. Welcome to **"Online Gold Rush:** Navigating the Road to Digital Wealth,"** your premier guide to financial success in the dynamic digital age.

This invaluable resource is your passport to prosperity, offering a meticulously charted path to financial freedom. It arms you with the precise insights and cutting-edge tools necessary to capitalize on the online landscape and supercharge your online earnings using the extraordinary capabilities of **ChatGPT**. Don't miss out on this exceptional opportunity to thrive in the digital era.

In a digital age brimming with opportunities, navigation is key. Each chapter serves as a stepping stone, expertly guiding you through vital aspects of online entrepreneurship while showcasing the remarkable prowess of **ChatGPT**.

Here's a glimpse of what awaits you:

Discover the Digital Landscape: Embark on your journey by exploring the limitless online opportunities available today. We'll help you set realistic expectations while emphasizing the crucial role of mindset and unwavering commitment.

Unleash the Power of ChatGPT: Dive deep into **ChatGPT's** capabilities and understand how it distinguishes itself from traditional AI and chatbots. Real-world examples will illuminate how businesses harness **ChatGPT** to achieve remarkable results.

Find Your Profitable Niche: Master the art of selecting a niche wisely, backed by comprehensive research into market demand and competition. Find your unique position in the market and stand out from the crowd.

Build an Irresistible Online Presence: Craft your professional online identity, from creating a captivating website to leveraging social media for audience engagement. Develop a compelling brand identity that resonates with your target audience.

Content is King: Learn the art of content creation with strategies for crafting a content plan, generating engaging material, and even using **ChatGPT** to spark ideas and draft content.

Monetize Your Content: Explore diverse monetization methods, including affiliate marketing, ads, and product sales. Discover how **ChatGPT-generated** content can elevate your revenue streams.

Grow Your Audience: Employ strategies to increase website traffic, build a valuable email list, and leverage **ChatGPT** to engage and expand your dedicated following.

Dominate Search Engines: Elevate your online visibility with essential search engine optimization (SEO) techniques. Leverage **ChatGPT** for keyword research and track and analyze your SEO performance.

Elevate Customer Support: Implement **ChatGPT** for handling customer inquiries, enhancing user experiences, and automating routine support tasks, ultimately boosting customer satisfaction.

Maximize Sales and Marketing: Utilize **ChatGPT** for lead generation, personalized marketing campaigns, and strategies aimed at enhancing conversion rates.

Elevate E-Commerce: Run a seamless online store with **ChatGPT's** assistance. Streamline product listings, descriptions, and efficiently manage inventory and order processing.

Data-Driven Decision Making: Understand the critical role of data analysis in online business and harness **ChatGPT** to extract insights for making informed strategic decisions.

Scale Your Online Business: Get ready for growth by delegating tasks and maintaining quality as you expand your online empire. Ensure scalability without compromising on excellence.

Overcome Challenges: Navigate the common obstacles faced by online entrepreneurs with strategies that emphasize resilience, adaptability, and ultimately, success.

Celebrate Success and Embrace the Future: Recognize your achievements, set new goals, and continually innovate and adapt in the ever-evolving online landscape.

With **"Online Gold Rush,"** your dreams of financial success in the digital realm are not merely dreams; they are tangible possibilities within your reach. This book serves as your ultimate guide to making money online using **ChatGPT**, and now is the time to embark on your journey toward digital wealth. Begin today, and let the digital gold rush transform your life. Your digital fortune awaits!

Foreword

In an era defined by innovation and relentless progress, our world is undergoing a remarkable transformation. Technology, particularly Artificial Intelligence (AI), is at the forefront of this revolution. It's with great excitement that I introduce you to "**Online Gold Rush**: Navigating the Road to Digital Wealth," a guide that explores the intersection of AI, **ChatGPT**, and the boundless opportunities of the digital age.

The need to make people aware of the current AI technology is pressing, for it is evolving at an astonishing pace. With each passing day, AI becomes more advanced, more accessible, and more integrated into our daily lives. The future belongs to those who understand its potential and seize the opportunities it presents.

This book is your compass in this rapidly evolving landscape. From the foundational Introduction to the Digital Gold Rush in Chapter 1, we embark on a journey through 15 chapters, each designed to empower you with the knowledge and strategies needed to thrive in the digital world.

In Chapter 2, we explore the remarkable capabilities of **ChatGPT**, clarifying how it differs from conventional AI and providing real-world success stories. Chapters 3 through 15 present an extensive guide to establishing a successful online business, covering everything from pinpointing your niche to expanding your operations. Throughout this journey, you'll uncover the indispensable role that **ChatGPT** plays in attaining digital prosperity.

In today's interconnected world, creating an online presence is not just a choice; it's a necessity. Chapter 4 explores the art of building a robust online presence, while Chapter 5 delves into content creation strategies with **ChatGPT** as your creative partner. Chapter 6 opens the door to monetization, and Chapter 7 reveals the secrets to growing your audience.

Furthermore, we explore SEO, data-driven decision-making, and the pivotal role of **ChatGPT** in enhancing customer support. Chapters 10 and 11 dive deep into the realms of sales, marketing, and e-commerce, all powered by **ChatGPT's** capabilities.

But it's not just about the destination; it's also about the journey. We address common challenges in Chapter 14, and in Chapter 15, we celebrate your achievements and set the stage for future horizons.

"**Online Gold Rush**" is more than a book; it's a tool for transformation. It's your ticket to navigate the road to digital wealth, leveraging the limitless potential of AI and **ChatGPT**. As the author, my aspiration is for you to not only gain knowledge but to use it as a catalyst for your own success.

So, welcome aboard this journey. Embrace the possibilities, embrace **ChatGPT**, and embrace your digital future. The gold rush is here, and your time to prosper is now.

Abdul Sami

Online Gold Rush

Chapter 1
Introduction to the Digital Gold Rush

An overview of the online opportunities available today

Setting realistic expectations for using ChatGPT to make money online

The importance of mindset and commitment

Navigating the Digital Gold Rush: Opportunities, Realism, and Mindset

In the vast landscape of the internet, a modern-day gold rush is taking place. The allure of digital wealth has captivated the aspirations of countless individuals, and for good reason. The online world has transformed into a thriving marketplace where fortunes are made, dreams realized, and limitless potential awaits.

Within this chapter, we embark on a journey of discovery, exploring the phenomenon of the digital gold rush and the extraordinary online opportunities available today. We also delve into the pivotal role that **ChatGPT** plays in this exhilarating landscape. Furthermore, we emphasize the importance of setting realistic expectations, nurturing the right mindset, and committing wholeheartedly to your online expedition.

The Landscape of Online Opportunities:

The digital age has ushered in a revolution that touches every aspect of our lives. It has not only altered our daily routines but also opened doors to a vast and ever-evolving world of online opportunities. Let's examine the diverse avenues this landscape offers:

E-Commerce: E-commerce is a prominent realm in the digital landscape, encompassing everything from running your online store to dropshipping or selling handcrafted goods on platforms like Etsy. With **ChatGPT**, you can enhance product listings, provide exceptional customer support, and craft compelling marketing content.

Example: Imagine you're a budding online entrepreneur selling handmade jewelry. **ChatGPT** can help you draft captivating product descriptions, automate customer inquiries, and even suggest personalized product recommendations based on customer preferences.

Content Creation: Content reigns supreme in the digital realm, spanning blogs, videos, podcasts, and social media. If you're passionate about a niche or possess unique skills, content creation can be your path to digital success. **ChatGPT** can assist by generating ideas, drafting articles, or crafting engaging social media posts.

Example: Suppose you're running a travel blog. **ChatGPT** can generate ideas for fresh travel content, write captivating destination guides, and even help create compelling social media updates to engage your audience.

Digital Marketing: The world of digital marketing is ever-expanding, with businesses seeking professionals well-versed in online advertising, SEO, and social media marketing. **ChatGPT** can provide valuable insights, devise marketing strategies, and craft persuasive ad copy.

Example: If you offer digital marketing services, **ChatGPT** can help you generate ad campaign ideas, optimize keywords for SEO, and create compelling ad copy that drives conversions for your clients.

Online Education: Online courses, webinars, and e-learning platforms have gained immense popularity. If you're an expert in a particular field, you can create and sell online courses. **ChatGPT** can assist in content creation, curriculum development, and even real-time interactions with students.

Example: Imagine you're a fitness trainer creating an online workout program. **ChatGPT** can help you develop course content, generate workout routines, and interact with participants to answer questions and provide guidance.

The emergence of **ChatGPT** has broadened horizons further, serving as an invaluable tool for entrepreneurs navigating this dynamic terrain. Its capabilities span content generation, idea generation, market research, and customer interaction, making it a versatile companion on your path to digital wealth.

What's most exciting is that these opportunities aren't reserved for a select few. The digital realm is remarkably democratic, accessible to anyone willing to embark on the journey. It's a realm where creativity, innovation, and hard work can pave the way to success, with **ChatGPT** as your guiding star.

Setting Realistic Expectations:

In the world of the digital gold rush, where stories of overnight success often dominate headlines, it's crucial to establish realistic expectations from the start. While the promise of rapid and extraordinary wealth can be alluring, it's essential to understand the realities of building a profitable online venture.

Time and Effort: Success in the digital realm, like any other endeavor, requires time and effort. Building and growing an online business is akin to nurturing a seed into a thriving plant. It demands consistent care, attention, and a commitment to learning and adapting. **ChatGPT**, while a powerful tool, doesn't circumvent the need for dedication and hard work.

Example: Consider a chef starting an online cooking course. Success won't happen overnight. It involves creating high-quality content, engaging with students, and continuously improving the course material.

Understanding Realistic Expectations: What can you genuinely expect from your endeavors with **ChatGPT** as your companion? Firstly, it's crucial to understand that **ChatGPT** is a powerful resource, but it operates within the framework of your goals and strategies. It can assist in content generation, idea brainstorming, and customer interactions, but it won't create an instant online empire.

Example: Imagine you're using **ChatGPT** to write blog posts for your online business. While **ChatGPT** can draft high-quality articles, it won't guarantee an immediate surge in website traffic or revenue. Success will depend on various factors, including content quality, SEO efforts, and audience engagement.

The Journey of Growth and Learning: Rather than viewing success as a destination, consider it a journey of growth and learning. **ChatGPT** can accelerate your progress, streamline processes, and provide insights, but it's the combination of your efforts and its capabilities that will yield results over time.

Example: Think of your online business as a garden. **ChatGPT** can be a powerful tool in tending to your garden by offering advice on caring for different plant varieties. However, it's your consistent effort, such as watering, pruning, and weeding, that will result in a flourishing garden over time.

Confidence and Resilience: By setting realistic expectations, you equip yourself with the confidence to persevere. Challenges and setbacks are part of the journey, not signs of failure. Instead, they are opportunities for learning and refinement. Your resilience in the face of adversity will be your greatest asset in the digital landscape.

Example: Consider an artist starting an online store to sell their artwork. They might encounter periods of slow sales or negative feedback. Realistic expectations allow them to view these moments as opportunities to improve their marketing strategies and product offerings, rather than as insurmountable obstacles.

Ultimately, managing your expectations involves finding the balance between optimism and pragmatism. It's about acknowledging the potential of **ChatGPT** as a tool that can enhance your digital wealth-building journey while recognizing that success demands persistence and adaptability.

The Mindset and Commitment:

In the ever-evolving and often unpredictable realm of the online world, your mindset and commitment emerge as your most invaluable assets on the journey to digital wealth. Success here isn't solely determined by having the right tools or resources; it's equally, if not more so, about having the right mindset.

Adaptability: The digital landscape is fluid, marked by constant change and innovation. To thrive, you must possess the ability to adapt to this ever-shifting terrain. Your mindset should be open to new ideas, technologies, and strategies. Embrace change as an opportunity rather than a challenge, and you'll find yourself at an advantage.

Example: Imagine you run a fashion e-commerce store. Embracing adaptability means you're open to incorporating new trends, exploring emerging marketing platforms, and adjusting your product offerings based on customer preferences.

Persistence: Challenges are a natural part of any entrepreneurial journey. Whether it's a downturn in business, a sudden algorithm change on a platform, or competition in your niche, persistence is the key to overcoming obstacles. A resilient mindset helps you persevere even when the path forward appears uncertain.

Example: Think of a software developer launching a new app. They may face unexpected technical issues or initial slow adoption. Persistence means they keep refining the app, seeking user feedback, and adapting it to meet evolving needs.

Continuous Improvement: The digital world rewards those who continually seek improvement. This means not settling for the status quo but constantly refining your skills, strategies, and offerings. A mindset of continuous learning and growth is essential for staying relevant and competitive.

Example: If you're a digital marketer, continuous improvement involves staying updated on the latest advertising platforms, refining your targeting strategies, and acquiring new skills like video marketing or data analysis.

Creativity: In a landscape as dynamic as the digital world, creativity is a powerful ally. It allows you to stand out, generate innovative solutions to problems, and connect with your audience on a deeper level. A creative mindset fosters innovation, enabling you to seize new opportunities as they arise.

Example: Imagine you manage a travel blog. A creative mindset inspires you to create unique travel itineraries, experiment with engaging video content, or design captivating social media campaigns to inspire wanderlust in your audience.

Unwavering Commitment: Commitment is the driving force that propels you forward, even when the journey becomes challenging. It's the unwavering dedication to your goals that keeps you focused on the prize, even in the face of setbacks. Commitment is the anchor that steadies your course in turbulent seas.

Example: Think of a startup founder launching a tech company. Their unwavering commitment means they work tirelessly to secure funding, build a talented team, and navigate market competition, even when faced with setbacks or market fluctuations.

As we embark on this journey through the digital gold rush, it's vital to understand that the landscape is vast and brimming with possibilities. With the right mindset, a commitment to your goals, and **ChatGPT** as your trusted companion, you are primed to explore and conquer the exciting world of online wealth creation.

In the pages that follow, we will not only dive deeper into the capabilities of **ChatGPT** but also unveil practical strategies for harnessing its power to build a profitable online business within six months. Together, we will navigate the road to digital wealth in the age of the **Online Gold Rush**, equipped with the mindset and commitment needed to thrive in this exhilarating digital frontier.

Chapter 2
The Power of ChatGPT

Understanding ChatGPT's capabilities and potential

How ChatGPT differs from traditional AI and chatbots

Real-world examples of businesses using ChatGPT effectively

Navigating the Digital Gold Rush: Opportunities, Realism, and Mindset

In the expansive domain of the internet, a contemporary rush for riches is underway. The allure of digital affluence has captured the imaginations of countless individuals, and the reasons for this fascination are readily apparent. The online realm has evolved into a vibrant marketplace where fortunes are forged, aspirations come to fruition, and limitless possibilities beckon.

Within this chapter, we shall embark on a voyage of discovery, delving into the phenomenon of the digital gold rush, the extraordinary online prospects of today, and the pivotal role that **ChatGPT** plays in this exhilarating landscape. Additionally, we will delve into the significance of establishing pragmatic expectations, nurturing the appropriate mindset, and pledging an unwavering dedication to your online expedition.

The Landscape of Online Opportunities

The digital age has revolutionized the way we live, work, and connect with the world. It has not only transformed our daily lives but also opened up a vast and dynamic landscape of online opportunities that hold the potential for individuals to achieve digital wealth. Let's take a closer look at what this landscape entails.

E-Commerce: One of the prominent realms within the digital landscape is e-commerce. It's the art of buying and selling products or services online. Whether you're running your online store, dropshipping, or selling handcrafted goods on platforms like Etsy, e-commerce offers an array of opportunities to generate income. With **ChatGPT**, you can enhance your product listings, provide better customer support, and create compelling marketing content.

Example: Imagine you're a budding online entrepreneur selling handmade jewelry. **ChatGPT** can help you draft captivating product descriptions, automate responses to customer inquiries, and even suggest personalized product recommendations based on customer preferences.

Content Creation: Content is king in the digital world, and it encompasses a wide spectrum of mediums, including blogs, videos, podcasts, and social media. If you're passionate about a particular topic or possess a unique skill, content creation can be your avenue to digital wealth. **ChatGPT** can assist by generating ideas, drafting articles, or even crafting engaging social media posts to boost your online presence.

Example: Suppose you're running a travel blog. **ChatGPT** can generate ideas for fresh travel content, write captivating destination guides, and even help create compelling social media updates to engage your audience.

Digital Marketing: The realm of digital marketing is ever-expanding. Businesses are constantly seeking professionals who can help them navigate the complex world of online advertising, search engine optimization (SEO), and social media marketing. With **ChatGPT**, you can offer valuable insights, devise marketing strategies, and craft compelling ad copy that drives conversions.

Example: If you offer digital marketing services, **ChatGPT** can help you generate ad campaign ideas, optimize keywords for SEO, and create persuasive ad copy that resonates with your target audience.

Online Education: The digital landscape has also redefined education. Online courses, webinars, and e-learning platforms have surged in popularity. If you have expertise in a particular field, you can create and sell online courses. **ChatGPT** can assist in content creation, curriculum development, and even interacting with students in real-time.

Example: Imagine you're a fitness trainer creating an online workout program. **ChatGPT** can help you develop course content, generate workout routines, and engage with participants by answering their questions and providing guidance.

The emergence of **ChatGPT** has further broadened these horizons. It serves as an invaluable tool for entrepreneurs and innovators seeking to navigate this ever-evolving terrain. Its capabilities extend to content generation, idea brainstorming, market research, and customer interaction, making it a versatile companion in the pursuit of digital wealth.

What's most exciting is that these opportunities are not confined to a select few. The digital realm is remarkably democratic; it's accessible to anyone willing to embark on the journey. It's a realm where creativity, innovation, and hard work can be the keys to success, and **ChatGPT** can be the guiding star on your path to digital prosperity.

As we continue our exploration, we'll delve deeper into how **ChatGPT** can be harnessed effectively across these diverse avenues, empowering you to make the most of the digital gold rush.

Setting Realistic Expectations

In the world of the digital gold rush, where stories of overnight success often grab headlines, it's imperative to establish realistic expectations from the outset. The allure of rapid and extraordinary wealth can be captivating, and the idea that **ChatGPT** could be a magic solution for instant riches might be tempting. However, it's essential to recognize the realities of building a profitable online venture.

Time and Effort: Success in the digital realm, just like any other endeavor, demands time and effort. The process of establishing and growing an online business is akin to nurturing a seed into a thriving plant. It requires consistent care, attention, and a commitment to learning and adapting. **ChatGPT**, while an extraordinary tool, is not a shortcut that circumvents the need for dedication and hard work.

Example: Consider a chef starting an online cooking course. Success won't happen overnight. It involves creating high-quality content, engaging with students, and continuously improving the course material.

Understanding Realistic Expectations: So, what can you realistically expect from your endeavors with **ChatGPT** as your companion? Firstly, it's crucial to understand that **ChatGPT** is a powerful resource, but it operates within the framework of your goals and strategies. It can assist in content generation, idea generation, and even customer interactions, but it won't create an instant and unassailable online empire.

Example: Imagine you're using **ChatGPT** to write blog posts for your online business. While **ChatGPT** can draft high-quality articles, it won't guarantee an immediate surge in website traffic or revenue. Success will depend on various factors, including content quality, SEO efforts, and audience engagement.

The Journey of Growth and Learning: Rather than viewing success as a destination, it's helpful to see it as a journey of growth and learning. **ChatGPT** can accelerate your progress, streamline your processes, and provide insights, but it's the amalgamation of your efforts and its capabilities that will yield results over time.

Example: Think of your online business as a garden. **ChatGPT** can be a powerful tool in tending to your garden by offering advice on caring for different plant varieties. However, it's your consistent effort, such as watering, pruning, and weeding, that will result in a flourishing garden over time.

Confidence and Resilience: By setting realistic expectations, you equip yourself with the confidence to persevere. You understand that challenges and setbacks are part of the journey, not signs of failure. Instead, they are opportunities for learning and refinement. Your resilience in the face of adversity will be your greatest asset in the digital landscape.

Example: Consider an artist starting an online store to sell their artwork. They might encounter periods of slow sales or negative feedback. Realistic expectations allow them to view these moments as opportunities to improve their marketing strategies and product offerings, rather than as insurmountable obstacles.

Ultimately, managing your expectations is about balancing optimism with pragmatism. It's about acknowledging the potential of **ChatGPT** as a tool that can enhance your digital wealth-building journey while recognizing that success will require persistence and a willingness to adapt.

In the chapters ahead, we'll delve deeper into practical strategies for harnessing **ChatGPT** effectively to achieve your online business goals. By understanding the symbiotic relationship between your efforts and **ChatGPT's** capabilities, you'll be well-prepared to navigate the digital landscape with the confidence and resilience needed to thrive.

The Mindset and Commitment

In the ever-evolving and often unpredictable realm of the online world, your mindset and commitment emerge as your most invaluable assets on the journey to digital wealth. Success here is not solely determined by having the right tools or resources; it's equally, if not more so, about having the right mindset.

Adaptability: The digital landscape is fluid, marked by constant change and innovation. To thrive, you must possess the ability to adapt to this ever-shifting terrain. Your mindset should be open to new ideas, technologies, and strategies. Embrace change as an opportunity rather than a challenge, and you'll find yourself at an advantage.

Example: Imagine you run a fashion e-commerce store. Embracing adaptability means you're open to incorporating new trends, exploring emerging marketing platforms, and adjusting your product offerings based on customer preferences.

Persistence: Challenges are a natural part of any entrepreneurial journey. Whether it's a downturn in business, a sudden algorithm change on a platform, or competition in your niche, persistence is the key to overcoming obstacles. A resilient mindset helps you persevere even when the path forward appears uncertain.

Example: Think of a software developer launching a new app. They may face unexpected technical issues or initial slow adoption. Persistence means they keep refining the app, seeking user feedback, and adapting it to meet evolving needs.

Continuous Improvement: The digital world rewards those who continually seek improvement. This means not settling for the status quo but constantly refining your skills, strategies, and offerings. A mindset of continuous learning and growth is essential for staying relevant and competitive.

Example: If you're a digital marketer, continuous improvement involves staying updated on the latest advertising platforms, refining your targeting strategies, and acquiring new skills like video marketing or data analysis.

Creativity: In a landscape as dynamic as the digital world, creativity is a powerful ally. It allows you to stand out, generate innovative solutions to problems, and connect with your audience on a deeper level. A creative mindset fosters innovation, enabling you to seize new opportunities as they arise.

Unwavering Commitment: Commitment is the driving force that propels you forward, even when the journey becomes challenging. It's the unwavering dedication to your goals that keeps you focused on the prize, even in the face of setbacks. Commitment is the anchor that steadies your course in turbulent seas.

Example: Think of a startup founder launching a tech company. Their unwavering commitment means they work tirelessly to secure funding, build a talented team, and navigate market competition, even when faced with setbacks or market fluctuations.

As we embark on this journey through the digital gold rush, it's vital to understand that the landscape is vast and brimming with possibilities. With the right mindset, a commitment to your goals, and **ChatGPT** as your trusted companion, you are primed to explore and conquer the exciting world of online wealth creation.

In the pages that follow, we will not only dive deeper into the capabilities of **ChatGPT** but also unveil practical strategies for harnessing its power to build a profitable online business within six months. Together, we will navigate the road to digital wealth in the age of the **Online Gold Rush**, equipped with the mindset and commitment needed to thrive in this exhilarating digital frontier.

Online Gold Rush

Chapter 3
Identifying Your Niche

Choosing a profitable niche or industry

Researching market demand and competition

Finding your unique angle in the market

Choosing a Profitable Niche or Industry

Selecting the right niche or industry in online business is a foundational decision that can significantly impact your journey towards success. Let's dive deeper into this critical aspect to understand its nuances:

Understanding Niches: A niche, in the context of online business, goes beyond being just a topic; it represents a specialized segment within a broader industry. To illustrate, consider the health and fitness industry. While "health and fitness" is the broader industry, niches within it could include "vegan nutrition for athletes" or "yoga for seniors." These niches are more specific, catering to distinct audiences. Niches can vary widely in their focus, ranging from broad to hyper-focused. By exploring various examples, we'll provide you with a clear understanding of how niches operate within the digital landscape.

Example: Imagine you're interested in the health and fitness industry. Instead of targeting the broad category, you narrow it down to a niche like "high-intensity interval training (HIIT) for busy professionals." This niche caters to a specific audience with unique fitness needs and preferences.

Profitability Analysis: Choosing a niche with the potential for profitability is paramount. Profitability in a niche is influenced by several factors, and we'll explore these in detail:

Market Size: Assessing the market size within your chosen niche is crucial. A larger market may offer more opportunities but also come with more competition. Conversely, a smaller niche might have less competition but potentially limited consumer demand. We'll discuss strategies for evaluating the market size to help you make informed decisions.

Example: Suppose you're considering entering the niche of "organic pet food." You would research the size of the market for organic pet food products, looking at factors like the number of pet owners interested in organic options.

Consumer Demand: Understanding the level of demand for products or services within your niche is vital. We'll delve into methods for researching and gauging consumer demand, ensuring you choose a niche with an audience willing to engage and spend.

Example: If you're exploring the niche of "eco-friendly home products," you'd want to research consumer interest in sustainable living and eco-friendly products, using tools like keyword research and surveys to assess demand.

Competition: Analyzing the competitive landscape is essential. We'll guide you through techniques for assessing the level of competition within a niche. Identifying niches with a healthy balance of demand and manageable competition can be a key to success.

Example: If you're considering the niche of "digital marketing for small businesses," you'd analyze the existing digital marketing agencies targeting small businesses, their services, pricing, and customer reviews to understand the competitive landscape.

Tools and Strategies: To facilitate your niche selection process, we'll introduce you to valuable tools and strategies. These resources will aid in researching potential niches, analyzing their profitability, and making data-driven decisions.

Example: Tools like Google Trends can help you identify trending topics within your niche, while competitor analysis tools can reveal insights into the strategies of other businesses in your chosen niche.

Passion vs. Profit: Striking a balance between your personal interests and profit potential is a fundamental consideration. While profit is important, aligning your niche with your passion can fuel long-term motivation and foster creativity. We'll delve into strategies for identifying niches that align with your interests and values. When your online business resonates with your passion, it becomes more than just a source of income; it becomes a fulfilling venture.

Example: If you have a deep passion for outdoor adventure, you might consider niches like "backpacking gear reviews" or "wilderness survival courses." Your enthusiasm for the niche will drive your content and engagement with your audience.

In summary, selecting a profitable niche involves understanding what niches are, conducting a comprehensive profitability analysis, and considering how your passions and interests can harmonize with your chosen niche. This thoughtful approach will set the stage for a successful online business venture.

Researching Market Demand and Competition

After identifying potential niches, the next crucial step is to conduct in-depth research to validate your choices. Let's delve deeper into this pivotal phase:

Market Research Tools: In this section, we will introduce you to a variety of powerful market research tools and techniques. These resources are essential for gaining insights into market demand, emerging trends, and consumer behavior. By utilizing these tools, you can access valuable data that informs your decisions about your chosen niche. We'll explore how to use these tools effectively to gather market data, identify trends, and gain a comprehensive understanding of your niche's dynamics.

Example: Tools like SEMrush can help you analyze competitors' websites, keywords, and backlinks, providing insights into their online strategies and audience engagement.

Competitor Analysis: Understanding your competition is an indispensable aspect of niche selection and business strategy. We'll guide you through the process of conducting competitive analysis. This entails researching and assessing your competitors within your chosen niche. We'll discuss strategies for identifying key competitors, analyzing their strengths and weaknesses, and uncovering the strategies they employ to reach their audience. By comprehensively understanding your competitors, you can devise strategies to differentiate yourself effectively.

Example: If you're entering the niche of "organic skincare products," competitor analysis would involve studying the websites, product offerings, customer reviews, and marketing strategies of established organic skincare brands.

Identifying Gaps: A potent strategy for standing out within your niche is to identify gaps or unmet needs in the market. We'll explore methods to pinpoint these opportunities for innovation and value creation. By identifying gaps, you can tailor your products or services to address specific needs that competitors may overlook. We'll delve into techniques for conducting gap analysis and demonstrate how it can lead to the development of unique selling propositions (USPs) that set your business apart.

Example: In the niche of "sustainable fashion," gap analysis might reveal a lack of affordable eco-friendly clothing options. This insight could lead you to launch a line of budget-friendly sustainable fashion products.

In essence, the research phase of niche selection involves harnessing market research tools, conducting thorough competitor analysis, and identifying gaps or unmet needs within your chosen niche. This process provides a solid foundation for crafting a business strategy that resonates with your target audience and positions your venture for success in the online marketplace.

Finding Your Unique Angle in the Market

In the digital realm, where competition is fierce, establishing a distinctive presence is the cornerstone of success. This section takes a closer look at strategies for carving out your unique position:

Brand Differentiation: Building a unique brand identity is essential for standing out in a crowded market. We'll dive into the intricacies of crafting a compelling brand identity, starting with the development of a captivating brand story. You'll learn how to define your brand's core values and create a visual identity that resonates deeply with your target audience. We'll also explore the significance of consistency in brand messaging and how it contributes to brand recognition and trust.

Example: If you're establishing a brand in the niche of "sustainable home decor," your brand story might revolve around your commitment to eco-friendly materials, ethical sourcing, and the positive impact of sustainable choices on the environment.

Content Strategy: Content is a potent tool for setting yourself apart from the competition. We'll delve into the art of developing a comprehensive content strategy that not only aligns with your chosen niche but also showcases your expertise. This includes creating content pillars that reflect your niche's core themes, establishing content calendars to maintain a consistent online presence, and crafting distribution plans to ensure your content reaches the right audience at the right time. We'll emphasize the importance of tailoring your content to your niche's specific interests and pain points.

Example: In the niche of "digital nomad lifestyle," your content strategy might include articles and videos on topics like remote work productivity, travel hacks, and personal stories of your digital nomad journey.

Unique Selling Proposition (USP): The concept of a Unique Selling Proposition (USP) is a critical element in differentiation. We'll explore the depth of USPs and guide you through the process of identifying precisely what sets your business or offerings apart from others in the market. By uncovering your USP, you'll gain a competitive edge and a clear messaging strategy that communicates your distinct value to your audience effectively.

Example: If you're operating in the niche of "healthy meal delivery," your USP might be "farm-to-table freshness" or "customizable meal plans tailored to individual dietary preferences."

By the end of this chapter, you'll have gained a comprehensive understanding of how to choose a profitable niche, conduct effective market research, and, most importantly, define your unique angle in the market. These foundational steps will not only set the stage for your success but also guide your journey toward digital wealth by enabling you to stand out and thrive in a dynamic and competitive online landscape.

Online Gold Rush

Chapter 4
Building a Strong
Online Presence

Creating a professional website or platform

Leveraging social media to connect with your audience

Crafting a compelling brand identity

Creating a Professional Website or Platform

In the digital age, your online presence serves as your storefront, office, and calling card, all rolled into one. This chapter is dedicated to the critical components of establishing and maintaining a robust online presence, which is a fundamental aspect of your journey toward digital wealth.

Website Essentials:
Your website or platform is the cornerstone of your online presence. In this section, we'll guide you through the essential elements of building a professional online home for your business:

Domain Selection: We'll start by unraveling the process of selecting the right domain name, which is essentially your web address. You'll learn how to choose a domain that aligns with your brand and is easy for your audience to remember.

Example: If your niche is gourmet coffee, a suitable domain might be something like "DeluxeBrews.com" – it's memorable and clearly related to your niche.

Hosting: Hosting is the virtual space where your website resides on the internet. We'll discuss the different hosting options available and help you select the one that suits your specific needs, whether it's shared hosting, VPS hosting, or dedicated hosting.

Example: If you anticipate high traffic and require advanced customization options, you might opt for VPS hosting to ensure your website's performance remains optimal.

Website Builders: For those without extensive technical knowledge, website builders can be a game-changer. We'll explore various website builder platforms and help you choose the one that aligns with your goals, whether you're building a simple blog or a complex e-commerce site.

Example: If you're starting a blog about sustainable living, platforms like WordPress or Squarespace could be ideal due to their user-friendly interfaces and blogging capabilities.

Design and User Experience:
The visual appeal and usability of your website are paramount to retaining and attracting visitors. In this part, we'll delve into the principles of user-friendly design, responsive layouts, and effective navigation. You'll discover how to create a website that not only looks great but also functions seamlessly across various devices.

User-Friendly Design: We'll explore design principles that enhance the user experience, such as the use of whitespace, clear typography, and the placement of essential elements for easy accessibility.

Example: A clutter-free homepage with intuitive navigation and readable fonts can make a significant difference in user experience.

Responsive Layouts: With the proliferation of smartphones and tablets, it's crucial that your website adapts to different screen sizes. We'll discuss responsive design techniques to ensure your site looks and works well on all devices.

Example: A responsive design ensures that your e-commerce store's product listings appear equally appealing and navigable on both desktop computers and mobile devices.

Optimizing Page Load Times: Slow-loading websites can turn visitors away. We'll provide tips and tools for optimizing your website's performance to ensure swift loading times.

Example: Compressing images and using content delivery networks (CDNs) can significantly improve page load times for image-heavy websites.

Content Creation:
Your website's content is the heart of your online presence, providing valuable information to your audience. We'll explore strategies for creating high-quality, engaging content that resonates with your target audience:

Structuring Blog Posts: Blogging is a powerful tool for connecting with your audience and establishing your expertise. We'll discuss how to structure your blog posts effectively, including the use of headings, subheadings, and engaging intros.

Example: If you're in the niche of tech reviews, structuring your posts with clear headings and sections for specifications, pros and cons, and a final verdict can enhance readability.

Compelling Product Descriptions: If you're running an e-commerce website, crafting compelling product descriptions is crucial for enticing customers. We'll delve into techniques for writing product descriptions that drive sales and conversions.

Example: For a jewelry e-commerce site, product descriptions that vividly describe materials, craftsmanship, and the story behind each piece can create an emotional connection with customers.

Multimedia Integration: In the age of multimedia, we'll also explore the integration of various media elements, such as images, videos, and infographics, to enhance your content and engage your audience effectively.

Example: In a cooking blog, including step-by-step recipe videos or mouthwatering food images can complement your written content and make it more engaging.

Leveraging Social Media to Connect with Your Audience

In the ever-evolving landscape of online marketing and engagement, social media has become an indispensable tool. In this section, we'll delve into how to effectively harness the power of social platforms to amplify your online presence and connect with your audience:

Platform Selection: Not all social media platforms are created equal, and each has its unique characteristics and user demographics. We'll discuss the major social platforms, such as Facebook, Instagram, Twitter, LinkedIn, and TikTok, and help you choose the ones that are most suitable for your business based on your niche and target audience.

Example: If you're offering professional coaching services, platforms like LinkedIn might be more beneficial for B2B networking and reaching a business-focused audience.

Platform Analysis: We'll provide insights into each platform's strengths and weaknesses, helping you make informed decisions about where to invest your time and resources. For instance, Instagram might be ideal for visually appealing products, while LinkedIn could be more suitable for B2B networking.

Example: If you're a fashion brand, Instagram's visual nature makes it a great platform for showcasing your products through high-quality images.

Content Strategy:
Effective social media marketing goes beyond posting random updates. Each social platform has its own dynamics, and understanding them is essential. We'll guide you through tailoring your content strategy for specific platforms:

Visual Content: On platforms like Instagram and Pinterest, visual content reigns supreme. We'll explore techniques for creating eye-catching images and graphics that grab users' attention and encourage engagement.

Example: A fashion brand can use Instagram to showcase new collections through visually appealing posts and stories.

Video Marketing: With the rise of video content, platforms like YouTube and TikTok offer immense potential. We'll discuss how to create compelling videos that tell your brand story, showcase your products or services, and connect with your audience on a personal level.

Example: A travel agency can use YouTube to share travel guides and vlogs, engaging viewers with exciting destination visuals.

Storytelling: Crafting compelling narratives is a universal strategy that transcends platforms. We'll delve into the art of storytelling and how to use it to resonate with your audience, evoke emotions, and build brand loyalty.

Example: A nonprofit organization can use storytelling on Facebook to share impactful stories of the individuals they've helped, fostering emotional connections with donors and supporters.

Audience Engagement:
Building a loyal following on social media is crucial for long-term success. We'll explore strategies for nurturing your social media community, turning followers into loyal advocates:

Community Management: Managing your social media community involves responding to comments, messages, and user-generated content. We'll discuss the importance of timely and authentic interactions to build trust and foster engagement.

Example: Responding promptly to customer inquiries on Twitter or addressing comments on your Instagram posts can demonstrate your commitment to customer satisfaction.

Hosting Live Events: Live streaming has gained popularity across various platforms. We'll explain how to leverage live events, webinars, and Q&A sessions to directly engage with your audience, answer questions, and showcase your expertise.

Example: A fitness trainer can host live workout sessions on Facebook or Instagram, encouraging real-time interaction with viewers.

User-Generated Content: Encouraging your audience to create content related to your brand can be a powerful strategy. We'll explore ways to inspire user-generated content and how to showcase it to boost authenticity and credibility.

Example: A restaurant can run a social media contest where customers share their food photos with a specific hashtag, creating a stream of user-generated content that highlights their delicious offerings.

Crafting a Compelling Brand Identity

In the digital realm, where competition is fierce and attention spans are short, a compelling brand identity can be the key to standing out. In this section, we'll delve into the art of crafting a brand identity that not only sets you apart but also resonates deeply with your target audience:

Brand Storytelling:
Stories have a unique power to connect with people emotionally. We'll guide you through the process of developing a brand narrative that captures the essence of your business and connects with your target market:

Identifying Your Story: We'll help you uncover the core story of your brand, whether it's the journey of your business, the problem you aim to solve, or the values you hold dear. This story will serve as the foundation of your brand identity.

Example: A craft brewery can craft a brand story around its founders' passion for brewing and commitment to using locally sourced ingredients.

Connecting with Emotions: Effective brand storytelling is about more than just facts; it's about evoking emotions. We'll explore storytelling techniques that help your audience connect with your brand on a personal level, creating a lasting impression.

Example: An outdoor adventure gear brand can use storytelling to convey the excitement and freedom of exploring the great outdoors with their products.

Visual Branding:
Your visual identity is the face of your brand. It encompasses elements like your logo, color scheme, typography, and imagery. We'll discuss how to create a cohesive and visually appealing brand identity that effectively communicates your brand's values and personality:

Logo Design: We'll delve into the principles of logo design, including simplicity, memorability, and versatility. You'll learn how to create a logo that not only looks great but also represents your brand effectively.

Example: A tech startup can design a sleek, modern logo that symbolizes innovation and simplicity.

Color Psychology: Colors evoke emotions and associations. We'll explore the psychology of colors and how to choose a color palette that aligns with your brand's message and resonates with your audience.

Example: A health and wellness brand might use calming blues and greens to convey a sense of tranquility and well-being.

Typography and Imagery: Typography and imagery play a crucial role in reinforcing your brand's identity. We'll provide tips on selecting fonts and images that complement your brand style and convey the right message.

Example: A luxury fashion brand might use elegant and sophisticated fonts in its marketing materials to align with its upscale image.

Consistency and Trust:
Consistency is a fundamental element in building trust and recognition. We'll delve into how to maintain a consistent brand voice and image across all your online touchpoints, from your website to your social media profiles:

Brand Guidelines: We'll discuss the creation of brand guidelines that outline the dos and don'ts of your brand identity. These guidelines ensure that your brand's visual and tonal consistency is maintained across all marketing materials and communications.

Example: Brand guidelines might specify the exact shade of blue used in your logo and provide guidelines on using your brand's tone of voice in social media captions.

Customer Trust: A consistent brand identity helps build trust with your audience. We'll explore how trust is essential in the digital age and how a well-defined brand identity contributes to this trust.

Example: When customers encounter a consistent brand image across various online channels, they are more likely to trust the brand's authenticity and reliability.

By the end of this chapter, you'll have the knowledge and tools to create a professional website, effectively leverage social media to connect with your audience, and craft a compelling brand identity. These elements will form the bedrock of your strong online presence, paving the way for success in the digital realm.

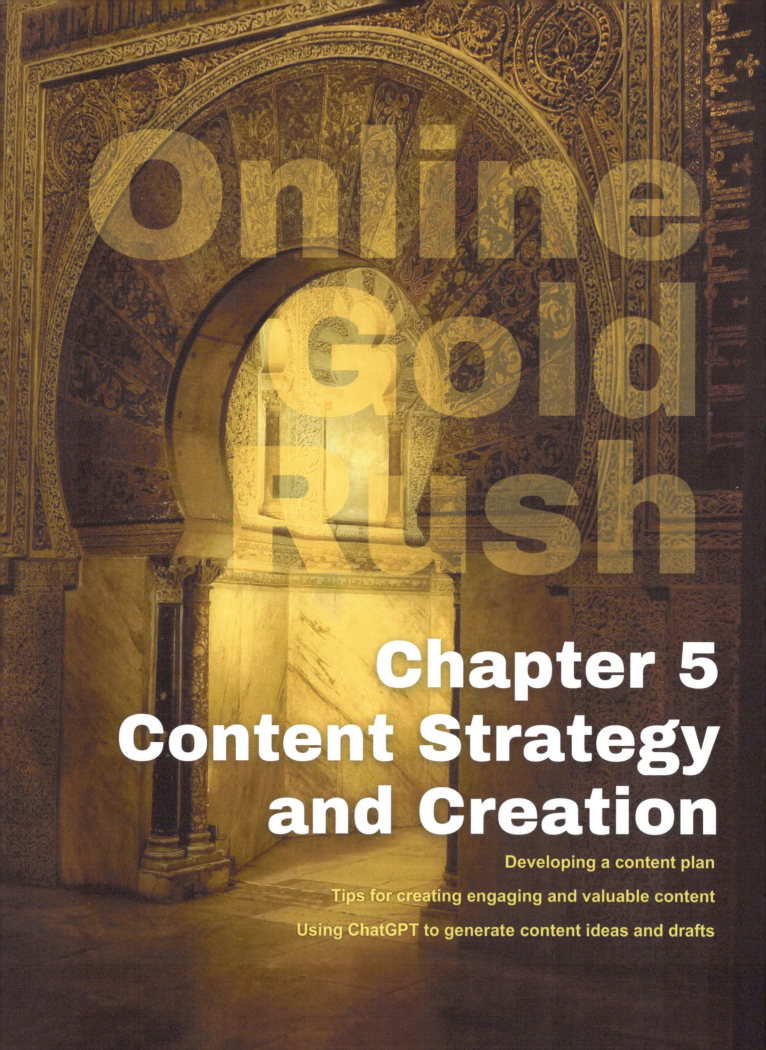

Online Gold Rush

Chapter 5
Content Strategy
and Creation

Developing a content plan

Tips for creating engaging and valuable content

Using ChatGPT to generate content ideas and drafts

Creating High-Quality and Engaging Content

Creating high-quality and engaging content is a cornerstone of success in the digital realm. In this chapter, we'll delve deep into crafting a robust content strategy, developing captivating content, and harnessing the power of **ChatGPT** to generate ideas and drafts.

Example: Let's say you're managing a lifestyle blog. Your content strategy should focus on creating visually appealing articles and videos that resonate with your audience's interests, such as fashion, travel, and wellness.

Developing a Content Plan

A well-structured content plan is the compass that guides your content creation efforts in the vast digital landscape. In this section, we'll explore the intricacies of developing a content plan that aligns with your niche, business goals, and audience preferences.

Example: Consider you're responsible for a startup's content strategy. Your plan should revolve around building brand awareness, attracting investors, and providing valuable insights into your industry, ensuring every piece of content contributes to these objectives.

Content Calendar

Planning Ahead: Consistency is the heartbeat of successful content marketing. Imagine you're running a travel blog. You know that your audience eagerly awaits travel tips every Friday. A content calendar helps you plan ahead and schedule your posts. This ensures that your audience receives a steady stream of valuable information and knows when to expect it.

Example: Suppose you operate a cooking website. Your content calendar can be structured around seasonal events, with special recipes and articles for holidays like Thanksgiving, Christmas, and Easter, aligning your content with your audience's culinary interests.

Aligning with Goals

Your content calendar should align with your business goals. If you're a software company aiming to establish thought leadership, your content calendar might include a series of in-depth technical articles, webinars, and whitepapers on relevant industry topics. This way, your content plan serves your objective of becoming an industry authority.

Example: If you manage a financial consultancy, your content calendar should align with the financial calendar, focusing on tax planning content in the months leading up to tax season and retirement planning articles as the year progresses, ensuring your audience receives timely and valuable information.

Content Goals:

Driving Traffic: If your primary goal is to attract more visitors to your website, you'll create content that appeals to search engines and social media algorithms.

For example, an e-commerce store selling outdoor gear might regularly publish articles about hiking and camping, capitalizing on SEO keywords and trending topics in the outdoor community.

Example: Consider a travel blog focusing on adventure travel. To drive traffic, you might create content about "Top 10 Must-Have Gadgets for Thrill-Seekers," optimizing it for relevant keywords like "adventure gear" and promoting it on social media platforms where outdoor enthusiasts gather.

Generating Leads: If lead generation is your focus, you'll delve into content types and tactics that encourage your audience to take action. Let's say you run a fitness coaching service. Your content plan could include downloadable workout guides and email sign-up incentives, providing valuable resources while capturing leads for your coaching programs.

Example: Imagine you're managing a real estate agency. To generate leads, you might offer downloadable guides like "The Ultimate Homebuyer's Handbook" or "Top Tips for Selling Your Property Faster." By collecting email addresses in exchange for these resources, you can build a list of potential clients.

Audience Research:
Understanding your target audience is at the core of effective content marketing. In this section, we'll dive deep into audience research techniques that help you uncover your audience's pain points, interests, and preferences.

Creating Buyer Personas: Buyer personas are detailed profiles representing your ideal customers. For a skincare brand, a buyer persona might be "Healthy Helen," a health-conscious woman in her 30s who values natural ingredients. Understanding Helen's needs and preferences helps tailor content, like blog posts on natural skincare routines and product recommendations, directly to her.

Example: Suppose you manage a pet supplies store. One of your buyer personas could be "Pet-Loving Patricia," a devoted pet owner who seeks high-quality, sustainable pet products. Crafting content that appeals to Patricia's values, such as articles on eco-friendly pet toys and organic pet food, can resonate with her and drive engagement.

Analyzing Data: Data and analytics provide insights into your audience's behavior and preferences. Suppose you run a technology blog. Analyzing data might reveal that your readers are particularly interested in product reviews and tutorials. Armed with this information, you can adjust your content plan to produce more of what your audience craves.

Example: If you operate a video game review website, data analysis might show that your audience engages more with reviews of role-playing games (RPGs).

You can respond by increasing the frequency of RPG reviews and creating related content like "Top RPGs of the Year" lists to further engage your readers.

Content Types:
Choosing Formats: Each content format has its strengths and applications. If you're a food blogger, you might utilize long-form articles with detailed recipes and step-by-step cooking instructions.

Example: Let's say you run a gardening blog. To engage your audience effectively, you could create content in various formats, such as "How-to Gardening Videos" demonstrating planting techniques and "In-Depth Gardening Guides" providing comprehensive advice on topics like soil preparation. This content diversity caters to both visual learners and readers.

Multichannel Approach: A multichannel content approach tailors content to the unique characteristics of each platform or medium you utilize. A fashion brand, for instance, might post high-resolution images of their latest collections on Instagram, create informative blog posts about fashion trends, and upload video tutorials on YouTube, appealing to different audience preferences and behaviors on each platform.

Example: Imagine you manage a health and wellness brand. To implement a multichannel approach, you could post motivational health quotes on Twitter, share in-depth articles on nutrition and fitness trends on your blog, and produce video content for platforms like TikTok where short, engaging health tips resonate with viewers.

Tips for Creating Engaging and Valuable Content:
Creating content that captures your audience's attention and provides genuine value is both an art and a science. In this section, we'll dive deeper into crafting content that is compelling, informative, and resonates with your audience.

Example: Suppose you operate a tech review website. To create engaging and valuable content, you might focus on in-depth product comparisons that highlight the pros and cons of various gadgets, helping your readers make informed purchase decisions. Additionally, incorporating user reviews and real-world usage scenarios can enhance the authenticity and value of your content.

Storytelling:
Connecting Emotionally: The power of storytelling cannot be overstated. Imagine you're a nonprofit organization dedicated to wildlife conservation. By sharing stories of successful rescue missions, like the heartwarming tale of rescuing a stranded baby sea turtle and releasing it back into the ocean, the emotional connection you create with your audience can lead to increased support and donations. Storytelling makes your content more relatable, memorable, and shareable.

Brand Consistency: Maintaining consistency in your brand's narrative across different pieces of content is crucial. If your brand is known for its commitment to sustainability, every piece of content should reflect this core value. For example, if you're an eco-friendly fashion brand, you can consistently convey your commitment to sustainability through content such as blog posts about eco-conscious fashion choices, videos showcasing sustainable manufacturing processes, and social media campaigns promoting eco-friendly fashion events.

SEO Optimization:

Keyword Research: Effective keyword research helps your content rank higher on search engine results pages. Suppose you run a digital marketing agency. In-depth keyword research can reveal valuable search terms like "content marketing strategies" or "social media advertising tips," which you can strategically incorporate into your content. For instance, you can create a comprehensive guide on "Effective Content Marketing Strategies" and ensure it includes these relevant keywords.

Optimization Techniques: SEO goes beyond keywords. Optimizing various elements of your content, from meta tags and headings to images and links, enhances your content's search engine rankings. Suppose you're an e-commerce site selling tech gadgets. Optimizing your product descriptions with clear, concise language, images, and relevant links improves the chances of appearing in search results for specific products. For example, you can optimize the product pages for your latest tech gadgets with high-quality images, well-structured headings, and links to related products and reviews, ensuring a seamless user experience for potential customers.

Engagement Techniques:

Interactive Content: Interactive content, such as quizzes, polls, and calculators, can significantly enhance user engagement. Suppose you're a financial advisor. Creating an interactive retirement savings calculator on your website allows visitors to input their financial data and receive personalized savings projections, actively involving them in the planning process. For instance, users can input their age, income, and savings goals to see how different scenarios impact their retirement plans, making your website a valuable resource for financial planning.

User-Generated Content: Leveraging user-generated content can create a sense of community and trust. If you operate a travel agency, encouraging customers to share their travel photos and stories on your website or social media can foster a community of travelers and build credibility. For example, a customer could post breathtaking photos from their recent trip to a remote island, accompanied by a detailed travelogue. This not only inspires other potential travelers but also showcases authentic experiences, making your travel agency a go-to choice for adventure seekers.

Visual Content:

Eye-catching Graphics: Effective visual content, such as infographics and graphics, conveys information effectively and enhances the overall look and feel of your content. Suppose you're an educational website focusing on history. Creating visually appealing timelines, maps, and infographics can make complex historical events more accessible and engaging for your audience. For instance, you can design an interactive historical timeline with engaging visuals, allowing users to explore different periods and events by clicking on specific points of interest, making history come alive.

Multimedia Elements: Images, videos, and audio play a crucial role in today's content landscape. Suppose you're a cooking blog. Captivating images of mouthwatering dishes, step-by-step recipe videos, and even audio clips of cooking tips and anecdotes can enrich your content and cater to diverse audience preferences. For example, you can create a video series where you demonstrate cooking techniques for various recipes while providing insightful commentary. These videos can complement your written recipes and engage users who prefer visual and auditory learning.

Using ChatGPT to Generate Content Ideas and Drafts:

Generating Ideas: Prompt Techniques: You can use **ChatGPT** effectively by providing specific prompts to spark creative ideas. For instance, you can ask open-ended questions like, "What are the latest trends in digital marketing?" to get insights and ideas for a blog post. **ChatGPT** can provide valuable topic suggestions and angles tailored to your niche. For instance, if you run a fashion blog, you can ask **ChatGPT** to suggest ideas for a post on upcoming fashion trends for the season, ensuring your content stays relevant and captivating.

Niche-Specific Topics: Tailoring your prompts to your niche is crucial. If you're in the technology sector, you might ask **ChatGPT** to generate content ideas related to emerging tech trends or tech product reviews. This ensures that the ideas generated are highly relevant to your target audience. For instance, you could request **ChatGPT** to provide insights into the latest advancements in artificial intelligence, helping you create content that resonates with your tech-savvy readers.

Overcoming Writer's Block: Writer's block can be a significant hurdle in content creation. **ChatGPT** can serve as a brainstorming partner, offering fresh angles and perspectives on familiar topics. For example, if you're writing about "digital marketing strategies," you can ask **ChatGPT** to provide unique approaches or case studies to inspire your content. Let's say you're stuck on a blog post about content promotion strategies; **ChatGPT** can suggest creative tactics like leveraging micro-influencers or hosting virtual events to boost your content's reach and impact.

Draft Creation:

Outlining Articles: ChatGPT can be your content outline generator. By asking it to outline an article, it can help you structure your content logically before you start writing.

If you're writing a guide on "Effective Email Marketing," **ChatGPT** can outline sections such as "Building an Email List," "Crafting Compelling Email Content," and "Measuring Email Campaign Success." This structured approach ensures that your content flows seamlessly, providing readers with a comprehensive guide to email marketing best practices.

Initial Drafts: If you need to kickstart an article or blog post, **ChatGPT** can assist in generating initial drafts. You can input prompts that encourage **ChatGPT** to provide comprehensive sections of content, which you can then refine and expand upon. For example, if you're writing a product review, **ChatGPT** can generate an initial section summarizing the product's features and benefits. This helps you jumpstart the writing process, ensuring that your review captures all essential details and highlights.

Refining Existing Content: Even if you have existing content, **ChatGPT** can help improve it. You can use **ChatGPT** to suggest edits, rephrase sentences for clarity, and provide additional insights or examples. If you have a blog post about "Healthy Eating Habits," **ChatGPT** can review and enhance it by suggesting statistics on the benefits of healthy eating or offering practical tips for meal planning. By enhancing your existing content, you can keep it up-to-date and more valuable to your audience.

Content Expansion:
In-Depth Explanations: **ChatGPT's** vast knowledge base makes it an excellent resource for expanding on topics. Suppose you have an article on "Artificial Intelligence in Healthcare." **ChatGPT** can provide in-depth explanations of AI applications in diagnostics, treatment, and healthcare administration, adding value and depth to your content. For instance, you can use **ChatGPT** to elaborate on the role of AI-powered diagnostic tools in early disease detection, making your healthcare article more informative and insightful.

Additional Sections: Sometimes, you may want to enrich your content by adding more sections or subtopics. If you're writing about "Green Energy Technologies," **ChatGPT** can generate sections on "Solar Energy Advancements" and "Wind Power Innovations," enhancing the comprehensiveness of your content. For example, **ChatGPT** can provide detailed information on the latest breakthroughs in solar panel technology and how they contribute to a sustainable future, ensuring your readers get a comprehensive overview of green energy solutions.

Enhancing Depth: **ChatGPT** can enhance the depth of your content by suggesting statistics, facts, and relevant examples. For a blog post about "Climate Change Impacts," **ChatGPT** can provide recent climate change statistics, real-world case studies of its effects, and examples of global initiatives addressing climate change. By incorporating this data and real-world context, your content becomes more authoritative and compelling, helping your audience better understand the urgency of climate change mitigation efforts.

Online Gold Rush

Chapter 6
Monetizing Your Content

Exploring various monetization methods (e.g., affiliate marketing, ads, product

sales)

Integrating ChatGPT-generated content into your strategy

Maximizing revenue streams

Monetizing Your Online Presence:
Monetizing your content is a crucial step in turning your online presence into a profitable venture. In this chapter, we'll explore various monetization methods, the integration of **ChatGPT-generated** content into your strategy, and strategies for maximizing your revenue streams.

Exploring Various Monetization Methods

Monetizing your online presence involves selecting the right revenue-generating strategies. In this section, we'll delve into four prominent monetization methods: affiliate marketing, ads, product sales, and sponsored content.

Affiliate Marketing:
Understanding Affiliate Marketing: Affiliate marketing involves promoting products or services from other companies through unique affiliate links. When a visitor to your platform clicks on the affiliate link and makes a purchase, you earn a commission.

Selecting Relevant Affiliate Programs: Let's say you run a technology blog. You might choose affiliate programs that align with your niche, such as promoting tech gadgets or software solutions. Researching and evaluating different programs helps determine their suitability.

Creating Effective Promotional Content: Crafting compelling content is essential for successful affiliate marketing. You could create in-depth product reviews, tutorials, or comparison articles that provide value to your audience while subtly promoting affiliate products.

Optimizing Your Strategy: Continuous optimization is key to maximizing your affiliate earnings. You might use analytics to track which affiliate links are performing best and refine your approach based on this data. Additionally, staying updated on industry trends can help you adapt to changes in the affiliate marketing landscape.

Ads:
Overview of Advertisements: Ads come in various formats, including display ads, native ads, and video ads. They generate revenue based on impressions, clicks, or specific actions. For instance, if you run a lifestyle blog, display ads might be a source of revenue when your audience clicks on them.

Exploring Ad Networks: Different ad networks offer various opportunities for revenue. You could delve into major ad networks like Google AdSense, exploring their advantages, requirements, and potential earnings.

Ad Placement Strategies: Proper ad placement can significantly impact revenue. Balancing user experience with revenue generation is crucial. For example, strategically placing ads within your content without overwhelming your readers can maximize earnings.

Ad Design Best Practices: Designing visually appealing and relevant ads is crucial for attracting user engagement. Ensure that your ads align with your content and blend seamlessly with your website's design to encourage clicks.

Product Sales:
Direct Monetization: Selling your products or services directly to your audience is a straightforward way to generate revenue through your online presence.

Product Creation: Let's say you offer online courses on digital marketing. You would need to create high-quality courses that resonate with your audience. Consider factors like course quality, pricing strategies, and efficient delivery methods.

E-commerce Platforms: Selecting the right e-commerce platform is vital. If you're selling physical products, platforms like Shopify can help you set up a user-friendly and secure online store. For digital products, platforms like Teachable can be suitable.

Leveraging Content for Sales: Your content can be a valuable asset in driving sales. For instance, if you're a fashion blogger, you could create content that showcases the clothing items you sell, providing styling tips and encouraging your audience to make purchases.

Sponsored Content:
Understanding Sponsored Content: Sponsored content involves brands paying you to create content that promotes their products or services. Maintaining transparency with your audience by clearly disclosing sponsored content is essential for credibility.

Identifying Sponsorship Opportunities: To identify potential sponsors, you might reach out to companies within your niche or leverage platforms that connect influencers with brands. Negotiating partnerships involves understanding the brand's expectations and deliverables for sponsored content.

Creating Authentic Sponsored Content: Crafting sponsored content that resonates with your audience while fulfilling the brand's objectives is crucial. You should aim to maintain authenticity and relevance in your sponsored posts. For example, if you're a travel influencer, sponsored travel diaries can authentically promote destinations and experiences.

Integrating ChatGPT-Generated Content into Your Strategy

Leveraging ChatGPT-generated content can be a valuable addition to your content strategy. This section explores three key aspects of integrating ChatGPT-generated content into your overall strategy:

Content Enhancement:
Complementing Existing Material: **ChatGPT** can assist in creating high-quality content that complements your existing content. For example, if you run a tech blog, **ChatGPT** can generate detailed explanations or FAQs to accompany your tech product reviews.

Maintaining Consistency: To maintain a consistent brand image, strategies for reviewing and editing **ChatGPT-generated** content are essential. Human oversight ensures that the content aligns seamlessly with your brand's voice, style, and messaging.

Quality Control: While **ChatGPT** can be a powerful content generator, human oversight is crucial for quality control. Editing and proofreading are necessary steps to ensure that **ChatGPT-generated** content meets your quality standards.

Content Automation:
Streamlining Content Creation: **ChatGPT** can automate specific content creation tasks, such as generating product descriptions, blog post outlines, or even brainstorming content ideas. This automation can save you valuable time and effort.

Customizing Automation: Customizing **ChatGPT's** automation to fit your specific needs involves setting up templates, defining input prompts, and configuring **ChatGPT** to generate content according to your requirements.

Optimizing Efficiency: By automating routine content creation tasks, you can increase your content production efficiency. Strategies for incorporating **ChatGPT** into your content creation workflow effectively can streamline your processes.

Content Personalization:
Understanding User Preferences: **ChatGPT** can help you tailor content to individual user preferences. Techniques for collecting and analyzing user data to understand their preferences, interests, and behavior are valuable.

Personalized Recommendations: Implementing chatbots powered by **ChatGPT** to offer personalized product recommendations or content suggestions to users can enhance user engagement and satisfaction.

Enhancing User Engagement: Personalization can significantly enhance user engagement and satisfaction. Delivering content that resonates with each user personally can lead to increased user retention and conversion rates.

Maximizing Revenue Streams

To ensure the profitability of your online presence, it's crucial to maximize your revenue streams. This section focuses on key strategies for achieving this goal:

Diversification:

Reducing Risk: Relying solely on one monetization method can be risky. Diversifying your income sources reduces dependency on one source and increases your income stability.

Exploring Multiple Avenues: Exploring various monetization methods simultaneously, such as affiliate marketing, ads, product sales, and sponsored content, creates a more robust and resilient income model.

Performance Tracking:

Continuous Monitoring: Effective monetization requires constant monitoring and optimization. Tools and techniques for tracking the performance of your monetization methods are essential.

Analytics: The use of analytics platforms to gain insights into user behavior, conversion rates, and revenue generation helps identify which monetization methods are most effective.

A/B Testing: A/B testing involves comparing different versions of your content or monetization strategies to optimize your revenue streams effectively.

Audience Engagement:

Fostering Loyalty: Engaging your audience can boost your monetization efforts. Techniques for building and maintaining a loyal audience, including email marketing, social media engagement, and user-generated content, are crucial.

Scaling:

Preparing for Growth: As your online presence grows, scaling your revenue streams becomes essential. Strategies for handling increased demand, maintaining quality, and scaling successful methods are discussed.

By the end of this chapter, you'll have a comprehensive understanding of various monetization methods, how to integrate **ChatGPT**-generated content into your strategy, and strategies for maximizing your revenue streams. Armed with this knowledge, you'll be better equipped to turn your online presence into a profitable endeavor and work towards your digital wealth goals.

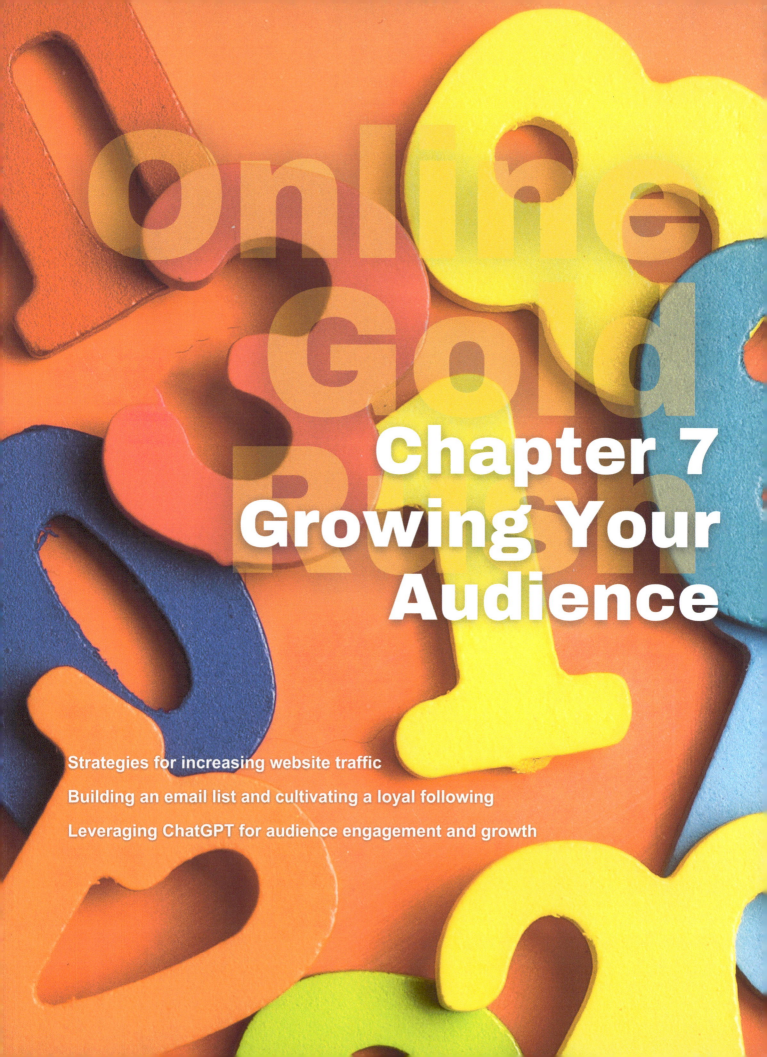

Chapter 7
Growing Your Audience

Strategies for increasing website traffic

Building an email list and cultivating a loyal following

Leveraging ChatGPT for audience engagement and growth

Strategies for Increasing Website Traffic

Growing your audience is crucial in the digital landscape. This chapter explores strategies for increasing website traffic, building an email list, cultivating a loyal following, and leveraging ChatGPT for audience engagement and growth:

Strategies for Increasing Website Traffic

Search Engine Optimization (SEO):
Keyword Research: Imagine you run a recipe blog. You can use SEO tools to identify high-traffic keywords related to recipes. For instance, "healthy breakfast recipes" could be a valuable keyword to target.

On-Page Optimization: To optimize your content, ensure that your recipe posts contain relevant keywords in titles, headings, and throughout the content. Use meta tags effectively to improve your ranking on search engine results pages (SERPs).

Backlink Building: Building quality backlinks is essential. Suppose you create a comprehensive guide on healthy eating. Outreach to nutrition websites to include your guide as a resource, generating valuable backlinks.

Content Marketing:
Blogging: Continuously publish informative and engaging blog posts related to your niche. For instance, if you have a travel website, regularly share travel guides, tips, and destination reviews.

Guest Posting: Collaborate with other reputable travel bloggers to write guest posts. These guest posts can include a link back to your website. This expands your reach and builds authority in the travel niche.

Creating Valuable Resources: Consider offering a free ebook on travel planning or downloadable checklists for packing. These resources provide value to visitors and encourage them to return to your site.

Social Media:
Platform Selection: If you're running a fashion blog, platforms like Instagram and Pinterest might be ideal for sharing visual content. Tailor your content to the platform that best suits your niche.

Content Promotion: Share your blog posts on social media with captivating visuals. Use relevant hashtags to reach a broader audience and encourage sharing among your followers.

Audience Engagement: Actively engage with your followers by responding to comments, asking questions, and hosting live Q&A sessions on platforms like Instagram or Facebook.

Paid Advertising:
Pay-Per-Click (PPC) Advertising: If you're selling fashion products, set up PPC ads targeting keywords like "online fashion store" to attract potential customers actively searching for fashion items.

Display Ads: Design visually appealing display ads showcasing your fashion products and run them on fashion-related websites to increase brand visibility.

Social Media Ads: Create engaging ad campaigns on platforms like Facebook and Instagram, targeting users based on their fashion interests and behavior.

Collaborations and Partnerships:
Influencer Collaborations: Partner with fashion influencers to showcase your products in their posts. For instance, collaborate with a well-known fashion influencer to feature your clothing line.

Business Partnerships: Collaborate with complementary businesses, such as jewelry or shoe retailers if you're in the fashion niche, to run joint promotions. This can introduce your website to their customer base.

Building an Email List and Cultivating a Loyal Following

Email Marketing:
Building an Email List: Offer incentives like exclusive fashion tips or early access to sales to encourage visitors to subscribe to your newsletter. Optimize subscription forms on your website for maximum conversions.

Segmentation: Segment your email list based on subscriber preferences. For example, segment subscribers interested in men's fashion separately from those interested in women's fashion. This allows for personalized content.

Email Campaigns: Send out newsletters with fashion trends, styling tips, and promotional offers. Create welcome sequences for new subscribers and run educational email campaigns about fashion.

Automation: Implement automated email sequences for abandoned cart recovery. When a visitor leaves items in their cart, send them automated emails with reminders and incentives to complete the purchase.

Engagement Strategies:
Webinars: Host webinars where you discuss fashion trends, styling tips, or sustainable fashion practices. This fosters engagement and positions you as an authority in the fashion niche.

Surveys: Conduct surveys to gather feedback on your fashion products, blog content, or user experience. Use insights from surveys to improve your offerings.

Contests: Organize fashion contests where participants can submit their unique fashion styles or designs. Offer attractive prizes to encourage participation.

Live Q&A Sessions: Host live question-and-answer sessions where your followers can ask fashion-related questions in real time, creating direct interactions.

Community Building:
Online Forums: Create fashion-related forums on your website where users can discuss trends, share outfit ideas, and seek fashion advice. Active participation can build a strong community.

Social Media Communities: Establish fashion communities on social media platforms where members can engage in discussions and share their fashion-related experiences.

Group Engagement: Actively engage with members of your fashion community by moderating discussions, organizing events like fashion challenges, and promoting inclusivity.

Leveraging ChatGPT for Audience Engagement and Growth

Chatbots for Support:
Enhanced User Experience: Implement **ChatGPT**-powered chatbots on your fashion e-commerce website to provide instant responses to customer inquiries, assisting with product selection and order tracking.

Inquiry Handling: Set up chatbots to handle common customer inquiries, such as sizing, shipping, and return policies, providing quick and accurate information.

Assistance and Guidance: Create chatbots that guide users through the fashion selection process by asking style preferences and suggesting suitable products.

Personalized Interactions:
Tailored Recommendations: Use **ChatGPT** to analyze user data and offer personalized fashion product recommendations, enhancing user engagement and increasing sales.

Content Customization: Customize responses and content based on user preferences and behavior, ensuring a more personalized and engaging user experience.

Content Expansion:
Interactive Quizzes: Develop interactive fashion quizzes that engage users while collecting data on their style preferences. This data can inform personalized product recommendations.

Chat-Based Courses: Create chat-based fashion courses or styling tutorials that provide valuable information in a conversational format, enhancing user engagement and learning.

Virtual Assistants: Use **ChatGPT** as a versatile virtual fashion assistant to answer user queries, suggest outfit combinations, and provide fashion tips.

Feedback and Surveys:
User Feedback: Utilize **ChatGPT** to collect user feedback on fashion products, website usability, or content quality. Use this feedback to make improvements and enhance user satisfaction.

Understanding User Needs: Conduct conversational surveys to gain insights into your audience's fashion preferences and needs, allowing you to tailor your fashion offerings accordingly.

By the end of this chapter, you'll have a comprehensive understanding of strategies for increasing website traffic, building an email list, cultivating a loyal following, and harnessing **ChatGPT** for audience engagement and growth. These insights empower you to expand your reach, connect with your audience on a deeper level, and drive your online venture toward digital wealth.

Online Gold Rush

Chapter 8
SEO and Online Visibility

Search engine optimization essentials

Using ChatGPT for keyword research and content optimization

Tracking and analyzing your SEO performance

Search Engine Optimization (SEO) Essentials

In today's digital landscape, achieving online visibility is paramount for the success of any online venture. This chapter explores critical aspects of SEO and how ChatGPT can enhance your website's visibility:

Understanding SEO:
Importance of SEO: Imagine you run a local bakery. SEO is crucial because it ensures that when someone searches for "best local bakery," your website appears in the top search results. This visibility can significantly impact your bakery's foot traffic and online orders.

Core Concepts: Understanding search engine algorithms, ranking factors, and user experience is fundamental. Google's algorithm, for example, considers factors like content quality, backlinks, and user engagement to rank websites.

Keyword Research:
Keyword Selection: Keyword research is like the compass of SEO. If you're running a tech blog, you might use tools to find keywords like "latest smartphone reviews" or "best laptops 2023."

Competitor Analysis: Analyzing your competitors can reveal keyword opportunities. If a rival tech blog is ranking well for "top gadgets," it's a keyword worth targeting.

On-Page Optimization:
Optimizing Web Pages: For your bakery website, optimizing the "Menu" page with descriptive titles and headers can help search engines understand your offerings better.

Content Optimization: Ensure that your bakery's "About Us" page has well-placed keywords, a coherent structure, and engaging content.

Content Quality:
High-Quality Content: Writing blog posts about unique cake recipes, sharing baking tips, or telling your bakery's story can not only attract search engines but also captivate your readers.

Link Building:
Backlinks: When a reputable food critic links to your bakery's website, it signals to search engines that your content is trustworthy.

Link Quality vs. Quantity: One high-quality backlink from a food magazine can be more valuable than many low-quality links from irrelevant websites.

Using ChatGPT for Keyword Research and Content Optimization

ChatGPT can be an ally in SEO tasks:

Keyword Generation:
Brainstorming Relevant Keywords: If you're launching a new menu, you can use **ChatGPT** to brainstorm keywords related to your new items. For instance, you could ask **ChatGPT**, "What are some keywords related to our new chocolate cake?"

Uncovering Popular Search Terms: To stay updated, you might ask, "What are the most popular cake flavors in 2023?" **ChatGPT** can provide insights based on recent trends.

Content Optimization:
Meta Description Refinement: **ChatGPT** can help refine meta descriptions for your bakery's products. For your "Chocolate Fondue Cake," **ChatGPT** could suggest a more enticing meta description to improve click-through rates.

Enhancing Content Structure: If you're writing a blog post about "Cake Decorating Tips," **ChatGPT** can provide recommendations on how to structure your headings and content sections for better readability and SEO.

Keyword Integration: **ChatGPT** can assist in naturally integrating keywords into your bakery's content. It can suggest where to place keywords and guide you on maintaining an appropriate keyword density.

Content Expansion:
Generating Additional Sections: If your bakery's "Wedding Cake" page lacks details, **ChatGPT** can help generate additional sections about cake customization options, flavors, and delivery details.

Comprehensiveness Impact: By expanding your content with **ChatGPT's** help, you can provide comprehensive information that appeals to both search engines and users.

Tracking and Analyzing Your SEO Performance

SEO Analytics Tools:
Google Analytics: You can use Google Analytics to track how many people visit your bakery's website and what pages they explore. For instance, you'll want to know if more users are viewing your "Wedding Cakes" page after optimizing it.

Google Search Console: This tool provides insights into how your bakery appears in Google search results. It's useful for monitoring your site's performance in searches related to "best local bakeries."

Key Metrics:
Organic Traffic: Monitoring organic traffic helps you gauge the impact of your SEO efforts. If you see a spike in visitors to your "Custom Cakes" page, it might be due to effective SEO.

Click-Through Rates (CTR): If you optimize your bakery's "Specialty Pies" page with compelling meta descriptions, you can track the CTR to measure the impact of those optimizations.

Bounce Rates: Reducing the bounce rate on your "Contact Us" page can be a goal. If visitors are leaving without contacting you, it may signal issues that need attention.

Conversion Rates: If your "Order Online" page has a low conversion rate, it might be time to analyze user behavior and optimize the page accordingly.

Data Analysis:
Identifying Trends: By analyzing your bakery's data, you might notice that searches for "gluten-free cupcakes" spike during certain months. This trend informs your content calendar.

Uncovering Areas for Improvement: If the "Cupcake Gallery" page has a high bounce rate, you can investigate why and make improvements.

Adapting Your Strategy: Based on data analysis, you can adapt your bakery's SEO strategy. If "cupcake delivery" keywords perform well, you might decide to offer a delivery service.

Competitor Analysis:
Assessing Competitor Strategies: You can analyze other local bakeries' websites. If a competitor's "Wedding Cakes" page ranks high, you can study their content and backlink strategy.

Refining Your Approach: Learning from competitors can help you refine your bakery's SEO approach. If they excel in local search results, you might focus on local SEO tactics.

By the end of this chapter, you'll have a comprehensive understanding of SEO essentials, how **ChatGPT** can assist in keyword research and content optimization, and strategies for tracking and analyzing your SEO performance. These skills are pivotal in improving your online visibility, attracting more organic traffic, and advancing on the path to digital wealth.

Online Gold Rush

Chapter 9
ChatGPT-Powered Customer Support

Implementing ChatGPT for customer inquiries

Enhancing user experience and satisfaction

Automating routine customer support tasks

Implementing ChatGPT for Customer Inquiries

Effective customer support is vital for any online business. Let's explore how ChatGPT can handle customer inquiries:

24/7 Availability:
Advantages of Round-the-Clock Access: Imagine you run an e-commerce website selling gadgets. **ChatGPT's** 24/7 availability ensures that customers can inquire about product specifications or track their orders at any time, leading to greater satisfaction.

Enhancing User Experience: It's midnight, and a customer wonders about a product's warranty. ChatGPT provides instant answers, making the user feel valued and fostering trust.

Handling Common Queries:
Creating a Knowledge Base: You can build a knowledge base containing product details, return policies, and troubleshooting guides. When a customer asks, "How can I return a faulty device?" **ChatGPT** can reference this knowledge base for accurate responses.

Training ChatGPT: Teach **ChatGPT** to recognize common customer inquiries. For instance, if customers often ask about product compatibility, ensure **ChatGPT** can provide relevant information.

Personalized Interactions:
Using Customer Data: By integrating **ChatGPT** with your CRM system, it can access customer information. When a frequent customer, John, asks for product recommendations, **ChatGPT** can offer suggestions based on John's previous purchases.

Addressing Customers by Name: Greeting customers by their names, e.g., "Hello, John," adds a personal touch. **ChatGPT** can use available data to address customers by name automatically.

Offering Tailored Recommendations: If a customer frequently buys hiking gear, **ChatGPT** can suggest new hiking products, enhancing the shopping experience.

Remembering Past Interactions: Imagine a customer asks for help with a product they previously inquired about. **ChatGPT** can recall past conversations, ensuring continuity. "Did you resolve the issue with your previous purchase?" This continuity improves user experience.

Enhancing User Experience and Satisfaction

Exceptional user experiences and customer satisfaction are paramount:

Natural Language Understanding:
Human-Like Fluency: ChatGPT's natural language processing ensures it understands and responds fluently. When a user asks, "How do I set up my new smartphone?" **ChatGPT** provides clear, concise instructions, reducing misunderstandings.

Improved Communication: Users appreciate conversing with a system that understands context. **ChatGPT's** context-aware responses create smoother interactions.

Multi-Language Support:
Overcoming Language Barriers: Your e-commerce platform can serve a global audience. **ChatGPT** can assist customers in multiple languages, fostering inclusivity.

Expanding Global Reach: By offering support in various languages, your business attracts diverse customers and demonstrates a commitment to a global audience.

Reducing Response Times:
Quick Response Times: Customers expect rapid responses. **ChatGPT** ensures they don't wait long for assistance. Quick answers improve user satisfaction.

Customer Expectations: In today's fast-paced digital world, customers expect instant responses. **ChatGPT's** efficiency meets these expectations, enhancing user experience.

Automating Routine Customer Support Tasks

Automation can significantly improve support efficiency:

Automated Responses:
Task Automation: **ChatGPT** can handle routine tasks like tracking orders, answering FAQs, or providing product information. When a customer asks, "Where is my order?" **ChatGPT** can fetch the tracking details.

Setting up Automation: Configure **ChatGPT** to recognize triggers or keywords. When a user mentions "order status," **ChatGPT** generates a predefined response. This frees human agents to focus on complex inquiries.

Ticket Routing:
Efficient Inquiry Handling: **ChatGPT** efficiently routes inquiries based on predefined criteria. For example, technical questions can be routed to the tech support team, ensuring customers receive expert assistance.

Customized Routing Rules: By creating custom rules, you ensure inquiries reach the right resources. For instance, if a customer mentions "defective product," **ChatGPT** can route the query to the quality control department.

Scalability:
Supporting Growth: As your business expands, **ChatGPT** can handle increased inquiry volumes without a proportional increase in costs. It's adaptable to growing workloads.

Efficient Scaling: To scale effectively, continually train **ChatGPT** on an expanding knowledge base and refine automation rules to accommodate new products or services.

Consistency: Automation ensures consistent responses, regardless of the inquiry volume or time of day. This consistency enhances user satisfaction.

Monitoring and Quality Assurance

Implementing **ChatGPT** in customer support requires continuous monitoring and quality assurance:

Performance Tracking:
Response Accuracy: Regularly monitor **ChatGPT's** responses for accuracy. Check if it provides the expected or desired answers. Metrics like the percentage of correct responses can measure accuracy.

Customer Feedback: Gather feedback from customers who interact with **ChatGPT**. Their insights help evaluate AI effectiveness and identify areas for improvement.

Identifying Improvement Areas: Analyze performance data to pinpoint areas where **ChatGPT** may underperform. For instance, if customers report misunderstandings in product descriptions, adjust **ChatGPT's** responses.

Human Oversight:
Balancing Automation and Human Intervention: Certain inquiries, like complex technical issues or emotional support, require human intervention. Establish protocols for human agents to step in when necessary.

Training and Feedback Loop: Train human agents to review AI-generated responses and provide feedback. This feedback loop helps refine **ChatGPT's** performance.

Ethical Considerations: Address potential biases in **ChatGPT's** responses, ensure data privacy, and maintain transparency with customers about AI usage.

Monitoring for Ethical Compliance: Regularly audit **ChatGPT's** interactions to identify inappropriate responses or privacy breaches and address them promptly.
By the end of this chapter, you'll understand how **ChatGPT** can be integrated into your customer support operations to enhance efficiency and user satisfaction, ensuring your online business delivers top-notch customer service.

Online Gold Rush

Chapter 10
ChatGPT in Sales and Marketing

Leveraging ChatGPT for lead generation

Creating personalized marketing campaigns

Closing sales and increasing conversion rates

Leveraging ChatGPT for Lead Generation

Lead generation is critical for business growth. Here's how ChatGPT can effectively contribute:

Engaging Landing Pages:
Integration: Imagine you run a real estate website. **ChatGPT** can be seamlessly integrated into property listings, engaging with visitors. Instead of static listings, **ChatGPT** can converse with potential buyers, offering assistance and insights.

Visitor Engagement: **ChatGPT** can initiate conversations by asking visitors about their preferences, budget, and desired location. It can then provide information on properties that match their criteria, effectively guiding them through the lead capture process.

Information Gathering: As visitors interact with **ChatGPT**, it can collect crucial information like contact details, preferred property types, and desired features. This data helps in tailoring follow-up communication.

Customized Recommendations: Based on visitor responses, **ChatGPT** can recommend specific properties that align with their preferences. For instance, if a user prefers a waterfront property, **ChatGPT** can highlight listings matching that criterion.

Qualifying Leads:
Lead Qualification Workflow: **ChatGPT** can assist in qualifying leads by asking targeted questions. For instance, it can inquire about the timeline for purchasing a property or specific property features a potential buyer is looking for.

Scoring Leads: Implement lead scoring based on user interactions. **ChatGPT** can automate this process by assigning scores to leads based on engagement level, budget, and other criteria.

Routing Leads: Once leads are qualified, **ChatGPT** can efficiently route them to the appropriate sales agents or brokers for further nurturing and conversion.

24/7 Lead Generation:
Continuous Availability: Unlike traditional methods, **ChatGPT** operates 24/7, ensuring that potential buyers can engage with your property listings and inquiries at any time. This constant availability maximizes lead capture opportunities.

Global Reach: **ChatGPT's** round-the-clock operation extends your lead generation efforts globally, attracting prospects from different time zones. This expanded reach can result in a higher volume of leads and conversions.

Reduced Response Times: Immediate responses to visitor inquiries, even during non-business hours, enhance the user experience and increase the likelihood of capturing leads before they lose interest.

Creating Personalized Marketing Campaigns

Personalization is key to effective marketing. ChatGPT can assist in crafting personalized campaigns:

Customer Segmentation:
Audience Understanding: Suppose you run an e-commerce fashion store. **ChatGPT** can analyze user interactions, preferences, and purchase history to segment your audience based on common characteristics, such as fashion style, budget, or preferred brands.

Dynamic Segmentation: **ChatGPT** continuously updates customer segments based on real-time data, ensuring that marketing campaigns are always aligned with the latest customer profiles.

Tailored Messaging: For each segment, **ChatGPT** can assist in generating personalized marketing messages that resonate with their unique preferences. For example, it can suggest clothing items based on past purchases.

Content Recommendations:
Behavior Analysis: **ChatGPT** can analyze user behavior, such as website visits and interactions with product listings. This data can be used to generate content recommendations that match each user's specific interests and needs.

Product Suggestions: For an online bookstore, **ChatGPT** can recommend books based on a user's reading history. If someone has shown an interest in mystery novels, **ChatGPT** can suggest the latest mystery releases.

Email Campaigns: In the context of email marketing, **ChatGPT** can assist in crafting personalized subject lines, email copy, and product recommendations tailored to each recipient's profile.

A/B Testing and Optimization:
A/B Test Ideas: **ChatGPT** can brainstorm A/B testing ideas for different elements of marketing campaigns. For instance, it can suggest variations for email subject lines or ad copy to test which versions yield the best results.

Optimization Suggestions: **ChatGPT** can provide insights based on A/B test results and ongoing performance analysis. It can generate recommendations for adjusting marketing strategies to improve conversions and engagement.

Data-Driven Insights: By analyzing user data and campaign performance, **ChatGPT** can generate insights into what is working and what needs improvement. It can provide recommendations for adjusting marketing strategies to align with user preferences and behaviors.

Closing Sales and Increasing Conversion Rates

Closing sales and boosting conversion rates are essential for business success:

Sales Assistance:
Product Knowledge: If you're running a software company, **ChatGPT** can serve as a virtual sales assistant by offering detailed information about your products. It can explain features, answer technical questions, and address user inquiries.

Objection Handling: **ChatGPT** can be trained to handle common objections or concerns. For instance, if a potential customer is concerned about software compatibility, **ChatGPT** can provide persuasive responses and suggest workarounds.

Product Recommendations: Based on user preferences and browsing history, **ChatGPT** can suggest relevant software packages or add-ons that align with the customer's needs.

Cross-Selling and Upselling: For an online electronics store, **ChatGPT** can identify opportunities for cross-selling by suggesting related accessories or upselling by highlighting premium features of a product.

Dynamic Pricing and Offers:
Personalized Pricing: **ChatGPT** can assist by providing dynamic pricing quotes based on user interactions and data. For example, it can offer personalized discounts or bundle pricing tailored to individual customers.

Limited-Time Offers: **ChatGPT** can create a sense of urgency by generating limited-time offers or promotions, emphasizing the benefits of acting quickly, such as cost savings or exclusive access to products.

Customized Bundles: If you run an online subscription box service, **ChatGPT** can suggest customized product bundles based on user preferences, encouraging customers to purchase multiple items at once.

Abandoned Cart Recovery:
Reminder Messages: **ChatGPT** can send automated reminder messages to users who have abandoned their shopping carts. These messages can include friendly reminders of the items left in the cart, along with persuasive language to encourage users to complete their purchases.

Incentives: To entice users to return to their abandoned carts, **ChatGPT** can offer incentives such as discounts, free shipping, or exclusive offers. These incentives sweeten the deal and motivate users to finalize their orders.

Assistance: If users encountered any issues during the checkout process, **ChatGPT** can provide assistance, addressing concerns, providing troubleshooting steps, and guiding users through the checkout steps.

Feedback and Iteration

Feedback and iteration are crucial for optimizing ChatGPT's performance:

Feedback Loops:
User Interaction Analysis: Regularly analyze user interactions with **ChatGPT** during sales and marketing activities. Identify common questions, challenges, and **ChatGPT's** responses.

Feedback Gathering: Actively collect feedback from users who have engaged with **ChatGPT**. Encourage users to share their experiences, both positive and negative.

Customer Support Feedback: Collaborate with your customer support team to gather insights from customers who have interacted with **ChatGPT**. They can provide valuable input on common issues and areas for improvement.

Internal Feedback: Seek feedback from internal team members who work closely with **ChatGPT**. Sales and marketing professionals, content creators, and developers may have valuable insights.

Iterative Enhancements:
Address Issues: Based on feedback, address issues and refine **ChatGPT's** responses and scripts to enhance its ability to assist users effectively.

Training Updates: If **ChatGPT** frequently struggles with specific questions or scenarios, consider updating its training data to better address those topics.

Monitoring and Analytics:
Implement Analytics Tools: Utilize analytics tools to track **ChatGPT's** impact on sales and conversion rates. Monitor user behavior, conversion funnels, and goals achieved through **ChatGPT** interactions.

Conversion Tracking: Set up conversion tracking to monitor the actions users take after engaging with **ChatGPT**. Track completed purchases, form submissions, or other desired actions.

ROI Analysis: Calculate the return on investment (ROI) for your **ChatGPT** implementation by comparing costs to revenue generated from **ChatGPT**-assisted sales and conversions.

A/B Testing: Implement A/B testing to compare **ChatGPT**-assisted interactions with non-assisted interactions. Determine which approaches yield the best results in terms of conversion rates and revenue.

User Feedback Integration: Incorporate user feedback and satisfaction scores into your analytics framework. Measure how user feedback correlates with conversion rates and sales outcomes.

Ethical Considerations

Ethical considerations are vital in ChatGPT's use for sales and marketing:

Transparency and Trust:
AI Usage Disclosure: Clearly disclose to users that they are interacting with an AI-powered system. Transparency builds trust and sets accurate expectations.

Data Privacy: Explain your data privacy policy, detailing how user data will be used, stored, and protected. Assure users that their information will be handled responsibly and in compliance with data protection regulations.

Consent Mechanisms: Implement clear consent mechanisms for users to agree to engage with **ChatGPT** and have their data processed for marketing and sales purposes.

User Control: Give users control over their interactions with **ChatGPT**, allowing them to pause or terminate conversations, delete their data, or adjust privacy settings.

Security Measures: Maintain robust security measures to protect user data from breaches or unauthorized access.

Bias Mitigation:
Bias Awareness: Recognize that AI models like **ChatGPT** can inherit biases. Be proactive in identifying potential biases and their implications for your sales and marketing content.

Bias Detection and Correction: Implement methods to detect and correct bias in **ChatGPT**-generated content. Refine the model's training data accordingly.

Diverse Training Data: Ensure that training data used for **ChatGPT** is diverse and representative, reducing the risk of perpetuating biases.

Continuous Monitoring: Regularly monitor **ChatGPT's** responses to assess whether it introduces bias or stereotypes.

Feedback Mechanisms: Encourage users to provide feedback regarding any biased or inappropriate responses they encounter while interacting with **ChatGPT**.

Ethical Guidelines: Develop and adhere to ethical guidelines for content generation, outlining what types of content are considered inappropriate or biased.

Bias Testing: Consider third-party audits to evaluate **ChatGPT's** performance for bias.

By the end of this chapter, you'll have a comprehensive understanding of how **ChatGPT** can be a game-changer in your sales and marketing efforts, from lead generation to personalized campaigns and increasing conversion rates, all while ensuring ethical and responsible AI use.

Chapter 11
ChatGPT in
E-Commerce

Running an online store with ChatGPT assistance

Streamlining product listings and descriptions

Managing inventory and order processing

Running an Online Store with ChatGPT Assistance

Running an online store with ChatGPT assistance can significantly enhance the shopping experience for your customers. Here's a detailed exploration of how ChatGPT can be leveraged:

Personalized Customer Experiences:
User Profiling: Imagine a clothing e-commerce store. **ChatGPT** can gather data about each customer's style preferences, past purchases, and browsing behavior. It can then use this data to provide personalized product recommendations. For instance, if a customer frequently buys casual wear, **ChatGPT** can suggest new arrivals in that category.

Recommendation Engines: Develop recommendation engines that leverage **ChatGPT** to analyze customer profiles. These engines can suggest products on various platforms, such as product pages, during checkout, or in personalized email campaigns. If a customer frequently buys outdoor gear, **ChatGPT** can recommend hiking boots when they visit the site.

Chat-Based Personal Shoppers: **ChatGPT** can act as a personal shopper. For example, if a customer asks, "What shoes would you recommend for a formal event?" **ChatGPT** can consider the event type, customer's style, and size to provide tailored suggestions, such as classic black leather shoes.

Virtual Shopping Assistants:
Product Search and Navigation: **ChatGPT** can assist customers in finding products efficiently. If a customer is looking for a specific brand of headphones, **ChatGPT** can refine search queries, apply filters, and guide them through product categories.

Product Information: Customers can ask **ChatGPT** about product specifications, materials, sizes, and more. **ChatGPT** can retrieve this information and present it in a conversational manner. For instance, if someone wants to know about camera specifications, **ChatGPT** can provide detailed answers.

Comparative Shopping: **ChatGPT** can compare products based on various attributes like price, features, and customer reviews. If a customer is torn between two smartphones, **ChatGPT** can provide a detailed comparison to aid in their decision-making process.

Inventory Updates:
Real-time Inventory Tracking: Implement a system that allows **ChatGPT** to access real-time inventory data. This ensures that **ChatGPT** can provide accurate information on product availability. For example, if a product is out of stock, **ChatGPT** can inform customers and provide an estimated restocking date.

Inventory Alerts: Set up **ChatGPT** to send alerts to subscribed customers when previously out-of-stock items become available again. This can re-engage customers who showed interest in those products but didn't make a purchase when they were out of stock.

Back-in-Stock Notifications: Customers can subscribe to receive back-in-stock notifications for specific products. **ChatGPT** can manage these subscriptions and send alerts as soon as the requested products are back in inventory, ensuring customers don't miss out.

Streamlining Product Listings and Descriptions

Effectively managing product listings and descriptions is crucial for attracting and converting customers. Here's a detailed exploration of how ChatGPT can streamline this process:

Product Descriptions:
Informative and Engaging Content: **ChatGPT** can generate product descriptions that not only provide essential information but also engage potential buyers. For instance, if you're selling smartphones, **ChatGPT** can highlight features like camera quality, battery life, and performance to make the product more appealing.

SEO Optimization: Incorporate relevant keywords and phrases into the product descriptions generated by **ChatGPT**. This ensures that your products rank higher in search results. For instance, if you're selling organic skincare products, **ChatGPT** can infuse product descriptions with relevant keywords like "natural skincare" or "organic beauty."

Customization: While **ChatGPT** can automate description generation, it's essential to review and customize the content. Tailor the descriptions to match your brand's style and voice, making any necessary edits for accuracy and consistency.

Content Generation:
User Reviews: Encourage customers to leave reviews, and use **ChatGPT** to assist in generating user reviews based on product feedback. These reviews enhance the credibility of your product listings and provide valuable insights to potential buyers.

FAQs: **ChatGPT** can help create an FAQ section for each product, addressing common questions and concerns that shoppers may have. This reduces the need for customers to contact support for clarifications.

Blog Posts: Use **ChatGPT** to generate blog posts that provide in-depth information about your products, industry trends, and related topics. This educates your audience and drives organic traffic to your e-commerce site. For instance, if you sell fitness equipment, **ChatGPT** can generate blog posts about home workouts and nutrition tips.

Consistency and Branding:
Brand Guidelines: Develop clear brand guidelines outlining your brand's tone, style, and messaging. Train **ChatGPT** to adhere to these guidelines, ensuring consistency in product listings and content generation.

Human Review: Implement a review process where human editors or content managers check the content generated by **ChatGPT**. This step helps maintain consistency, verify accuracy, and align the content with your brand's voice.

Template Usage: Create templates for product listings and descriptions with placeholders for essential information. **ChatGPT** can populate these templates with relevant content while adhering to the established format and style.

Managing Inventory and Order Processing

Efficiently managing inventory and order processing is vital for any e-commerce business. Here's an in-depth look at how **ChatGPT** can assist in these areas:

Automated Inventory Management:
Stock Level Tracking: **ChatGPT** can monitor and track your inventory levels in real-time. It can provide regular updates on product availability and alert you when stock levels are running low, helping you avoid stockouts.

Demand Prediction: By analyzing historical data and customer behavior, **ChatGPT** can provide insights into demand trends. This information can be used for inventory planning and restocking decisions.

Low Stock Notifications: When products are close to running out of stock, **ChatGPT** can automatically notify you and suggest reordering specific quantities to maintain optimal stock levels.

Order Processing and Tracking:
Order Status Updates: **ChatGPT** can provide customers with real-time order status updates. Customers can inquire about the status of their orders, and **ChatGPT** can provide information about whether the order is processing, shipped, or out for delivery.

Estimated Delivery Times: **ChatGPT** can estimate delivery times based on shipping methods and locations. It can also provide customers with tracking information for their orders, enabling them to monitor the progress of their deliveries.

Handling Customer Inquiries: **ChatGPT** can assist in handling common customer inquiries related to orders, such as order modifications, cancellations, or address changes. This ensures that customers receive prompt and accurate responses.

Returns and Refunds:
Return Process Assistance: **ChatGPT** can guide customers through the returns process, explaining the steps they need to follow and the required documentation. It can also assist in generating return labels for customers.

Refund Inquiries: When customers inquire about refunds, **ChatGPT** can provide information on the refund timeline and process. It can also address common questions about refund policies and eligibility.

Handling Exception Cases: While **ChatGPT** can manage routine return and refund requests, it's essential to have human oversight for complex or exceptional cases that require personalized attention or decisions outside the standard procedures.

Scaling Your E-Commerce Business

As your e-commerce business experiences growth, scaling your operations effectively becomes paramount to ensure continued success. In this context, **ChatGPT** can be a valuable asset in several key areas:

Scaling Strategies: Implementing scalable strategies is essential to accommodate larger volumes of sales, inquiries, and inventory management. **ChatGPT** can assist in automating various aspects of your business, such as customer support, order processing, and inventory management. It can also help maintain consistent and personalized customer experiences as your business expands.

Managing Larger Inventories: With business growth often comes an increased product inventory. **ChatGPT** can aid in automating inventory management tasks, including tracking stock levels, predicting demand trends, and notifying customers about low stock. This ensures that you can efficiently handle larger product catalogs without compromising customer satisfaction.

Handling Increased Customer Inquiries: As your customer base grows, so does the volume of inquiries. **ChatGPT** can efficiently handle a higher number of customer queries, providing quick responses and assistance 24/7. It can also assist in categorizing inquiries and routing them to the appropriate departments or support agents, ensuring efficient problem resolution.

International Expansion: If you plan to expand your e-commerce business internationally, **ChatGPT** can play a pivotal role. It can provide multilingual support to engage with customers in different languages, helping you tap into global markets. Additionally, its round-the-clock availability ensures that customers from various time zones receive timely assistance, enhancing their shopping experience.

Ethical Considerations in E-Commerce AI Integration

Integrating AI, like **ChatGPT**, into your e-commerce operations offers numerous benefits, but it also raises ethical considerations that must be addressed to maintain trust and protect customer interests. Here are two crucial ethical aspects to consider:

Transparency in AI Assistance:
Clearly disclose the use of AI: Make it evident to customers that they are interacting with an AI system. You can use chatbot disclaimers or messages to inform users that they are conversing with AI technology.

Set realistic expectations: Ensure that customers understand the capabilities and limitations of **ChatGPT**. Make it clear that while it can provide helpful information and support, it may not replace human assistance for certain complex inquiries.

Privacy and Security:
Protect customer data: Handling customer data and transaction information securely is paramount. Implement robust data protection measures to safeguard sensitive information.

Data encryption: Use encryption protocols to protect data in transit and at rest. This ensures that customer data remains confidential during transactions and interactions.
Compliance with data protection regulations: Adhere to relevant data protection regulations, such as GDPR or CCPA, to ensure that customer privacy rights are respected.

Data retention policies: Establish clear data retention policies to determine how long customer data will be stored. Dispose of data that is no longer needed to reduce the risk of data breaches.

Regular security audits: Conduct routine security audits and assessments to identify vulnerabilities and address potential threats promptly.

By the end of this chapter, you'll have a comprehensive understanding of how **ChatGPT** can transform your e-commerce operations. From enhancing the customer experience to streamlining product management and order processing, **ChatGPT** can help you run a more efficient and customer-centric online store in the competitive world of e-commerce.

Online Gold Rush

Chapter 12
Analytics and
Data-Driven
Decision Making

The importance of data analysis in online business

Utilizing ChatGPT for data extraction and insights

Making informed strategic choices

Ethical Considerations in E-Commerce AI Integration

Integrating AI, like ChatGPT, into your e-commerce operations offers numerous benefits, but it also raises ethical considerations that must be addressed to maintain trust and protect customer interests. Here are two crucial ethical aspects to consider:

Transparency in AI Assistance:
Transparency is fundamental when using AI in e-commerce interactions. Customers have the right to know when they are engaging with AI-powered systems like **ChatGPT**.

Example: Imagine a customer initiates a chat on your e-commerce website to inquire about product recommendations. In this case, it's essential to have a clear message at the beginning of the conversation stating, "You are chatting with an AI-powered assistant that can provide product recommendations."

Set Realistic Expectations: In addition to disclosing the use of AI, it's crucial to set realistic expectations. Make it clear that while **ChatGPT** can provide helpful information and support, it may not replace human assistance for certain complex inquiries. For example, inform customers that **ChatGPT** may not handle highly technical questions but can assist with general product information.

Privacy and Security:
Protecting customer data is of utmost importance in e-commerce operations. Handling customer data and transaction information securely is paramount.

Data Encryption: Implement strong encryption protocols to protect data in transit and at rest. This ensures that customer data remains confidential during transactions and interactions. For instance, all customer data and payment information should be encrypted to prevent unauthorized access.

Compliance with Data Protection Regulations: Adhere to relevant data protection regulations, such as GDPR (General Data Protection Regulation) or CCPA (California Consumer Privacy Act), to ensure that customer privacy rights are respected. This involves obtaining proper consent for data collection and processing and providing customers with clear privacy policies.

Data Retention Policies: Establish clear data retention policies to determine how long customer data will be stored. Dispose of data that is no longer needed to reduce the risk of data breaches. For example, if customer data is retained for marketing purposes, clearly communicate how long it will be stored and allow customers to opt out.

Regular Security Audits: Conduct routine security audits and assessments to identify vulnerabilities and address potential threats promptly. Regularly update security measures to stay ahead of evolving cybersecurity threats.

Utilizing ChatGPT for Data Extraction and Insights

In today's data-driven world, extracting valuable insights from various sources is crucial for informed decision-making and staying competitive. ChatGPT can be a powerful tool for data extraction and analysis. Here's a detailed look at how you can leverage ChatGPT for these purposes:

Data Extraction:
ChatGPT can assist in extracting valuable information from unstructured data sources, turning raw data into actionable insights.

Example: Consider an e-commerce store that receives a high volume of customer reviews. **ChatGPT** can be tasked with extracting common themes, sentiments, and key feedback from these reviews. For instance, **ChatGPT** can identify recurring issues like shipping delays or product quality concerns.

Natural Language Processing (NLP): **ChatGPT's** natural language processing capabilities make it adept at understanding and summarizing large volumes of text data. This is particularly valuable for analyzing customer feedback and conducting sentiment analysis.

Market Research: **ChatGPT** can also serve as a valuable tool for conducting market research by summarizing industry reports, news articles, and market trends. For instance, **ChatGPT** can analyze and summarize the latest industry reports on consumer electronics trends.

Making Informed Strategic Choices with Data Analysis and ChatGPT

To make informed strategic choices in your online business, you can employ a data-driven decision-making framework, utilize **ChatGPT** for personalization and customer insights, and leverage A/B testing and optimization techniques. Here's a more detailed explanation of these components:

Data-Driven Decision-Making Framework:
Establishing a data-driven decision-making framework involves several key steps:
Data Collection: Begin by collecting relevant data from various sources, such as customer interactions, website analytics, sales data, and market research. For example, collect data on website traffic, conversion rates, and customer demographics.

Data Analysis: Use analytical tools, including **ChatGPT** for text analysis, to process and analyze the data. Identify patterns, trends, and correlations that can inform your strategic choices.

Interpretation: Translate the data-driven insights into actionable strategies. Understand the implications of the data on your business goals and objectives.

Decision Implementation: Execute the strategic choices based on the insights gained from data analysis. This may involve adjustments to marketing campaigns, product offerings, customer experiences, or operational processes.

Monitoring and Feedback: Continuously monitor the impact of your decisions and gather feedback. Use ongoing data analysis to refine and optimize your strategies over time.

Personalization and Customer Insights:
ChatGPT can assist in creating personalized customer experiences by leveraging data-driven insights:

Customer Segmentation: Use data analysis to segment your customer base according to preferences, behaviors, demographics, or purchase history. For example, identify high-value customers who frequently purchase premium products.

Behavior Analysis: Analyze customer behaviors and interactions with your business to understand their needs, pain points, and preferences. For instance, analyze click-through rates on specific product categories to identify popular items.

Content Recommendations: Utilize **ChatGPT** to suggest relevant products, services, or content to individual customers based on their profiles and past interactions. For example, recommend complementary products to customers based on their previous purchases.

Tailored Marketing: Craft personalized marketing messages and campaigns that resonate with specific customer segments. For instance, send targeted email offers to customers who have abandoned their shopping carts.

A/B Testing and Optimization:
A/B testing is a powerful method for optimizing various aspects of your online business:

Hypothesis Generation: Use **ChatGPT** to generate hypotheses for A/B tests. For example, **ChatGPT** can suggest alternative ad copy, email subject lines, or website content for testing.

Test Execution: Implement A/B tests to compare two or more variants of a webpage, marketing email, or other elements to determine which performs better. For instance, test different product page layouts to see which results in higher conversion rates.

Results Analysis: Analyze the data from A/B tests to understand which variant leads to better outcomes, such as higher conversion rates or increased customer engagement. For example, analyze click-through rates and conversion rates for different email campaign variants.

Iterative Optimization: Use the insights from A/B testing to iteratively optimize your strategies. Implement changes based on what you've learned to continually improve results. For example, adjust the timing of email campaigns based on when customers are most likely to open and click.

Continuous Improvement with Data Analysis and ChatGPT

Continuous improvement is a fundamental aspect of leveraging data analysis and ChatGPT to enhance your business operations and decision-making. Here's a more detailed look at how you can ensure ongoing progress and success:

Iterative Data Analysis:
Understand that data analysis is not a one-time task; it's an ongoing and iterative process.

Data Collection: Continue to collect relevant data from various sources, including customer feedback, sales data, website analytics, and more.

Data Cleaning: Ensure that the data you collect is accurate, complete, and free from errors. Regularly clean and preprocess data to maintain its quality.

Data Analysis: Use tools, including **ChatGPT**, to analyze data and derive insights. Monitor key performance indicators (KPIs) and metrics to identify trends, opportunities, and areas for improvement.

Data Visualization: Visualize data through charts, graphs, and dashboards to make it more accessible and understandable for stakeholders.

Feedback Integration: Incorporate insights gained from data analysis into your business strategies and operations. Make data-driven decisions to drive improvements.

Case Studies:
Learning from real-world case studies can provide valuable insights into how businesses have successfully leveraged data analysis and **ChatGPT** to drive growth and improve customer experiences.

Example: Explore a case study of an e-commerce company that used data analysis to identify a bottleneck in its checkout process. By optimizing the checkout flow based on data insights, they achieved a significant increase in conversion rates.

Common Themes: Some common themes in case studies might include customer segmentation, product optimization, operational efficiency, and marketing effectiveness.

By the end of this chapter, you'll be equipped with the knowledge and tools to harness the power of data analysis and **ChatGPT** for data extraction and insights. You'll also understand how to apply data-driven decision-making principles to steer your online business toward success. Data is not just information; it's the fuel that drives informed, strategic choices in the digital age.

Online Gold Rush

Chapter 13
Scaling Your
Online Business

Preparing for growth and expansion

Outsourcing tasks and delegating responsibilities

Maintaining quality as you scale

Outsourcing Tasks and Delegating Responsibilities for Business Scaling

Outsourcing and delegation are vital strategies for business scaling. Let's delve into the details of how these processes work effectively:

The Power of Delegation:
Understanding Delegation's Importance: Delegation is crucial for business growth as it allows you, as a business owner or leader, to focus on high-priority tasks that require your expertise. Delegating routine or time-consuming tasks frees up your time and energy for strategic decision-making and business development.

Example: Consider a small e-commerce startup. The founder initially manages customer support, product sourcing, and marketing. As the business grows, they realize that handling customer inquiries is taking up too much time. By delegating customer support to a dedicated team, the founder can now concentrate on product expansion and market strategy.

Identifying Delegable Tasks: To effectively delegate, identify tasks that can be outsourced without compromising quality or your business's core functions. These tasks often include administrative work, customer support, content creation, and specific technical tasks.

Example: In an e-commerce business, tasks like data entry, order processing, and inventory management can be delegated to employees or outsourced partners, allowing the core team to focus on product development and marketing.

Finding the Right Talent:
Hiring and Partnering Strategies: Determine whether you need to hire full-time employees, collaborate with freelancers, or engage with specialized agencies. Consider your business's current needs, budget, and long-term goals when making these decisions.

Example: A growing e-commerce store may choose to hire full-time customer support representatives to handle increasing customer inquiries. Simultaneously, they might outsource graphic design tasks to freelance designers for periodic marketing campaigns.

Recruitment Process: Implement a structured recruitment process to find the right talent. This includes defining job roles and responsibilities, creating detailed job descriptions, conducting interviews, and checking references. Hiring platforms and agencies can also be valuable resources for talent acquisition.

Example: When hiring customer support representatives, conduct interviews that assess communication skills, problem-solving abilities, and product knowledge. Check references to ensure the candidates have a history of providing excellent customer service.

Building a High-Performing Team: Once you've assembled your team, focus on team building, fostering a positive work culture, and providing ongoing training and development to ensure your workforce remains efficient and motivated.

Example: In an e-commerce company, organizing team-building activities like problem-solving workshops or product knowledge sharing sessions can help create a cohesive and motivated customer support team.

Effective Delegation:
Clear Expectations: When delegating tasks, it's crucial to set clear expectations for your team members. Clearly communicate the task's objectives, deadlines, quality standards, and any specific instructions.

Example: If you're delegating the task of creating product descriptions for an e-commerce website, provide guidelines on word count, tone, and style, and set deadlines for each batch of descriptions.

Proper Training: Ensure that team members have the necessary skills and knowledge to perform their delegated tasks effectively. Provide training, access to resources, and ongoing support as needed.

Example: If you're delegating the management of your e-commerce store's social media accounts, offer training on the brand's voice, content calendar, and tools for scheduling posts.

Accountability and Communication: Establish systems for accountability, such as regular progress updates, milestones, and performance evaluations. Maintain open lines of communication to address questions, concerns, or challenges that may arise during task execution.

Example: In an e-commerce business, set up regular team meetings to discuss progress, share insights, and address any issues that customer support representatives may encounter while dealing with customer inquiries.

Risk Mitigation:
Data Security: When outsourcing tasks that involve sensitive data, implement robust data security measures. This includes data encryption, secure file sharing, and non-disclosure agreements to protect confidential information.

Example: If you're outsourcing the management of customer payment information, ensure that the payment gateway used is secure, and sensitive data is encrypted both in transit and at rest.

Quality Control: Develop quality control processes to monitor the work of outsourced individuals or teams. Regularly review their output, provide feedback, and make necessary adjustments to maintain quality standards.

Example: In a scenario where product photography is outsourced, establish quality control checkpoints to ensure that the images meet the desired standards in terms of clarity, lighting, and composition.

Legal Considerations: Understand the legal aspects of outsourcing, including contracts, intellectual property rights, and compliance with labor laws. Consult legal experts to ensure that your outsourcing arrangements are legally sound.

Example: When outsourcing software development for an e-commerce platform, ensure that the contract clearly defines ownership of code, intellectual property rights, and any non-compete clauses to protect your business interests.

Maintaining Quality as You Scale Your Business

Maintaining quality is crucial as your business scales. Here are detailed insights into how to ensure quality as you grow:

Quality Assurance Systems:
Processes and Standards: Implement standardized processes and quality standards for every aspect of your business operations, from product development to customer service. Document these processes comprehensively to ensure consistency.

Example: In an e-commerce business, create standardized procedures for product quality checks before shipping. Document these procedures to ensure that every team member follows the same checklist.

Quality Control Tools: Utilize quality control tools and methodologies to monitor and improve your products or services. Tools like Six Sigma, Lean, and Total Quality Management can help you identify areas for improvement and eliminate defects.

Example: In an e-commerce logistics department, implement Six Sigma principles to reduce shipping errors by analyzing data and identifying root causes of mistakes in order fulfillment.

Customer-Centric Approach:
Customer Satisfaction Metrics: Continuously measure customer satisfaction through metrics like Net Promoter Score (NPS), customer feedback surveys, and online reviews. Use these insights to identify areas where your business can enhance the customer experience.

Example: An e-commerce store can regularly send post-purchase surveys to customers to gauge their satisfaction with the ordering process, shipping speed, and product quality.

Customer Support: Invest in robust customer support systems to handle increased demand as you scale. Provide training to support teams to maintain a high level of service quality and responsiveness.

Example: In a rapidly growing e-commerce business, expand your customer support team and provide comprehensive training on product knowledge and effective communication to ensure consistent quality in resolving customer inquiries.

Feedback Loops:
Customer Feedback: Actively gather customer feedback through various channels, including surveys, social media, and direct interactions. Analyze this feedback to identify pain points and areas where you can make improvements.

Example: An e-commerce platform can use social media listening tools to track customer sentiment and identify trending issues, allowing them to proactively address concerns.

Employee Input: Encourage your employees to provide feedback on processes and customer interactions. They often have valuable insights into areas that can be streamlined or enhanced.

Example: In an e-commerce warehouse, warehouse staff may provide input on optimizing the fulfillment process to reduce shipping errors and improve efficiency.

Stakeholder Engagement: Engage with stakeholders such as suppliers, partners, and investors to gather their perspectives on your business's quality and performance. Their feedback can provide valuable insights.

Example: Collaborate with key suppliers to discuss ways to improve the quality of raw materials used in your e-commerce product manufacturing, leading to a higher-quality end product.

Data-Driven Decision-Making:
Collect and Analyze Data: Collect and analyze data related to quality metrics, customer satisfaction, and operational efficiency. Use data-driven insights to make informed decisions about process improvements and scaling strategies.

Example: Analyze customer feedback data to identify recurring issues with a product and use this information to drive product improvements and quality enhancements.

Continuous Improvement: Embrace a culture of continuous improvement, where every team member is encouraged to suggest enhancements and contribute to maintaining or elevating quality standards.

Example: In an e-commerce business, create a dedicated channel or platform where employees can submit suggestions for process improvements or quality enhancements, and recognize and reward innovative ideas.

Resource Allocation:
Scalable Resources: Ensure that your resources, including human resources, technology, and infrastructure, can scale proportionally with your business. This prevents overstretching resources and maintains quality during growth.

Example: As an e-commerce business grows, invest in scalable web hosting solutions to accommodate increased website traffic without compromising loading speeds or user experience.

Training and Development:
Employee Training: Provide ongoing training and development opportunities for your workforce. This helps employees adapt to new challenges and technologies, ensuring they can continue to deliver high-quality work as your business evolves.

Example: In an e-commerce company, offer employees access to e-learning platforms to enhance their skills in areas like digital marketing, customer service, or data analysis.

Risk Management:
Risk Assessment: Continually assess potential risks that could impact the quality of your products or services. Develop contingency plans to mitigate these risks and ensure business continuity.

Example: In an e-commerce business heavily reliant on overseas suppliers, create a risk management plan that includes alternative sourcing options to address supply chain disruptions.

Legal and Compliance:
Regulatory Compliance: Stay updated on relevant industry regulations and compliance requirements. Ensure that your operations and products adhere to these standards to avoid legal issues and penalties as your business scales.

Example: In the cosmetics e-commerce industry, ensure that product labeling complies with FDA regulations, and regularly review and update product formulations to meet evolving standards.

Documentation and Knowledge Management:
Document Everything: Maintain comprehensive documentation of your processes, standards, and best practices. This documentation is invaluable for training new employees and ensuring consistency.

Example: Document the step-by-step process of conducting quality checks for products in your e-commerce business, including checklists, guidelines, and visual references.

Leveraging Technology and Automation for Scaling

Scaling a business often goes hand in hand with leveraging technology and automation. Here's a detailed exploration of how technology, including ChatGPT and other AI tools, can enhance efficiency and how data management plays a crucial role:

Leveraging Technology:
Process Automation: Identify repetitive and time-consuming tasks within your operations, such as data entry, order processing, or customer inquiries. Implement automation solutions, like **ChatGPT**-powered chatbots, to handle these tasks efficiently.

Example: An e-commerce business can use AI chatbots to handle routine customer inquiries, such as order tracking or return requests, freeing up customer support agents to focus on complex issues.

Workflow Optimization: Use technology to optimize workflows. Employ project management software, task automation tools, and collaboration platforms to enhance teamwork, task assignment, and project tracking.

Example: Implement project management software that tracks the progress of new product launches in an e-commerce company, ensuring that all tasks are completed on schedule.

Customer Engagement: Leverage AI-driven personalization tools to enhance customer engagement. AI can analyze customer data to suggest tailored product recommendations, send personalized marketing emails, and even provide real-time support through chatbots.

Example: An e-commerce website can use AI algorithms to analyze a customer's browsing and purchase history to suggest related products, increasing cross-selling and upselling opportunities.

Data Management:
Data Collection and Storage: With business growth, data accumulates rapidly. Implement robust data collection and storage strategies to ensure you can capture and access valuable information when needed. Invest in scalable and secure data storage solutions, such as cloud-based databases.

Example: As an e-commerce business expands, it can migrate its data storage to a cloud-based platform to accommodate the increasing volume of customer data while ensuring data accessibility and security.

Data Security: Prioritize data security to protect sensitive customer and business data. Implement encryption, access controls, and regular security audits to safeguard information from breaches and cyber attacks.

Example: Implement end-to-end encryption for customer payment information, ensuring that financial data remains secure during online transactions.

Analytics and Business Intelligence: Utilize data analytics tools to gain insights into customer behavior, market trends, and operational performance. These insights can guide strategic decisions and help you identify opportunities for improvement.

Example: Analyze website traffic and sales data to identify peak shopping hours in an e-commerce business, allowing you to optimize marketing campaigns and inventory management accordingly.

AI and Machine Learning: Explore AI and machine learning applications for data analysis. These technologies can uncover patterns and trends that humans might miss, offering a competitive advantage in understanding market dynamics and customer preferences.

Example: Use machine learning algorithms to predict customer preferences and trends in an e-commerce business, enabling proactive inventory management and product recommendations.

Scalable Systems: Ensure that your data management systems can scale seamlessly with your business. Scalability is essential to handle growing data volumes without compromising performance or data integrity.

Example: Invest in a scalable Customer Relationship Management (CRM) system that can accommodate the addition of thousands of new customer records as your e-commerce business expands.

Integration and Interoperability:
Integrate Systems: Integrate various software and systems across your business operations for seamless data flow. For example, integrate your e-commerce platform with inventory management, accounting, and CRM systems to ensure data consistency and accuracy.

Example: Integrate your e-commerce website with a shipping management system to automate order fulfillment, update tracking information, and enhance the customer experience.

APIs and Middleware: Leverage APIs (Application Programming Interfaces) and middleware solutions to connect different software applications. This integration simplifies data sharing and improves efficiency.

Example: Use APIs to connect your e-commerce store with payment gateways, allowing for secure and efficient payment processing.

Customization: Tailor technology solutions to your specific Customization ensures that the technology you implement aligns with your business processes and goals.

Training and User Adoption:
Employee Training: Provide comprehensive training to employees to ensure they can effectively use new technologies and automation tools. Training should cover both basic and advanced functionalities.

Example: Train employees on the use of inventory management software in an e-commerce business, including features for tracking stock levels, generating purchase orders, and managing vendor relationships.

User Adoption: Encourage user adoption by involving employees in the technology selection process. Gather their input and feedback to address concerns and facilitate a smoother transition.

Example: When implementing a new Customer Relationship Management (CRM) system in an e-commerce company, involve the sales and customer support teams in the selection process to ensure the chosen system meets their needs.

Scalability and Future-Proofing:
Scalable Solutions: Choose technology solutions that are scalable, meaning they can grow with your business. Scalability minimizes the need for frequent technology overhauls as you expand.

Example: Select a scalable e-commerce platform that can handle increased website traffic and product listings as your business grows without significant code changes.

Stay Current: Stay updated on technological advancements and industry trends to ensure your business remains competitive. Regularly assess your technology stack and make upgrades or adjustments as needed.

Example: In the fast-paced world of e-commerce, stay informed about emerging trends in online shopping behavior, such as mobile commerce or social commerce, and adapt your technology strategies accordingly.

Scaling Challenges and Pitfalls

Scaling a business presents numerous challenges and pitfalls that, if not addressed effectively, can hinder growth and even lead to setbacks. Here's a detailed exploration of common challenges and the importance of learning from case studies:

Common Challenges:
Overexpansion: One of the most common pitfalls is overexpansion, where a business grows too quickly without the necessary resources, infrastructure, or customer demand to support it. This can strain finances, lead to operational inefficiencies, and dilute the quality of products or services.

Example: An e-commerce startup rapidly expands its product catalog without conducting market research, leading to excess inventory and strained cash flow.

Resource Constraints: As a business scales, it often faces resource constraints, especially in areas like capital, skilled labor, and technology. Balancing the need for investment with financial stability is crucial.

Example: An e-commerce company experiences rapid growth but struggles to hire enough skilled developers to maintain its website, leading to performance issues and customer frustration.

Cultural Shifts: Scaling often necessitates a cultural shift within the organization. Maintaining the company's core values and culture while adapting to growth can be challenging. Ensuring that employees remain aligned with the company's mission is essential.

Example: A small, tight-knit e-commerce team expands rapidly, and the founder notices a shift in the company's culture. To address this, they implement team-building activities to maintain the original collaborative spirit.

Market Saturation: In some industries, scaling can lead to market saturation, where competition intensifies and profit margins narrow. Businesses must continually innovate and differentiate themselves to thrive.

Example: An e-commerce business faces increased competition in the fashion industry, requiring it to introduce unique product lines and marketing strategies to stand out.

Scalability of Processes: Not all processes are inherently scalable. Some may need to be redesigned to accommodate growth. Ensuring that key processes can scale smoothly is vital.

Example: An e-commerce company realizes that its manual order fulfillment process cannot keep up with increased order volumes. It invests in an automated warehouse system to improve scalability.

Customer Satisfaction: Maintaining high levels of customer satisfaction can become challenging as the customer base grows. Consistently delivering quality products or services and providing excellent customer support is critical.

Example: An e-commerce store receives complaints about delayed customer support response times due to increased inquiries. It hires additional support staff and implements a ticketing system to improve response efficiency.

Case Studies:

Successful Scaling: Analyze case studies of businesses that successfully scaled to identify strategies and best practices. Learn how they navigated challenges, adapted their business models, and maintained quality while growing. For example, companies like Amazon, Netflix, and Airbnb have undergone significant scaling and can offer valuable insights.

Example: Studying Amazon's expansion from an online bookstore to a global e-commerce and cloud computing giant can provide insights into scaling strategies, including diversification and technology innovation.

Challenges and Failures: Similarly, study case studies of businesses that faced challenges or even failed during scaling attempts. Analyze the reasons behind their setbacks, including financial mismanagement, inadequate market research, or poor resource allocation. Understanding these pitfalls can help you avoid making similar mistakes.

Example: Examining the downfall of a once-promising e-commerce startup that expanded too quickly and neglected customer feedback can reveal the importance of measured growth and continuous improvement.

Sustainability and Long-Term Growth

Sustainability is increasingly becoming a critical consideration for businesses as they scale. Here's a more detailed exploration of sustainability in the context of long-term growth:

Environmental and Social Impact: As your business grows, it has a broader environmental and social footprint. Sustainable practices involve minimizing negative impacts, such as reducing carbon emissions, conserving resources, and promoting social responsibility. These practices not only align with ethical principles but can also enhance your brand reputation.

Example: An e-commerce company commits to reducing its carbon footprint by optimizing shipping routes to minimize fuel consumption and using eco-friendly packaging materials.

Long-Term Viability: Sustainable business practices contribute to the long-term viability of your company. By adopting environmentally friendly technologies, optimizing resource usage, and engaging in social responsibility initiatives, you reduce operational costs, increase efficiency, and attract environmentally conscious customers and investors.

Example: A sustainable e-commerce business invests in solar panels to power its warehouses, reducing energy costs and aligning with renewable energy goals.

Brand Reputation: Sustainable practices can enhance your brand reputation. Consumers increasingly favor eco-friendly and socially responsible brands. Demonstrating a commitment to sustainability can differentiate your business in a competitive market and lead to brand loyalty.

Example: An e-commerce fashion retailer gains a loyal customer following by exclusively selling clothing made from sustainable and ethically sourced materials.

Regulatory Compliance: Many regions have introduced regulations related to sustainability and environmental responsibility. Staying compliant with these regulations is essential to avoid legal issues and penalties as your business scales.

Example: An e-commerce company operating in Europe ensures compliance with the EU's Single-Use Plastics Directive by phasing out single-use plastic packaging and adopting reusable and recyclable alternatives.

Innovation and Efficiency: Sustainability often drives innovation and efficiency. It encourages businesses to seek eco-friendly alternatives, optimize supply chains, and reduce waste. These innovations can lead to cost savings and improved competitiveness.

Example: An e-commerce electronics retailer introduces a take-back program for old electronic devices, promoting recycling and refurbishing to reduce electronic waste and open new revenue streams.

Transparency: Communicate your sustainability efforts transparently to customers, investors, and stakeholders. Transparency builds trust and demonstrates your commitment to responsible business practices.

Example: An e-commerce company publishes an annual sustainability report detailing its efforts to reduce its environmental impact, showcasing achievements and setting future goals.

Sustainable Supply Chains: Consider the sustainability of your supply chain. Work with suppliers who share your commitment to sustainability, and ensure that the sourcing of materials aligns with ethical and environmental standards.

Example: An e-commerce company sources organic cotton for its clothing products and partners with Fair Trade-certified manufacturers to ensure fair wages and ethical working conditions.

By the end of this chapter, you'll have a comprehensive understanding of the strategies, considerations, and challenges associated with scaling your online business. Whether you're preparing for rapid expansion or gradual growth, the insights and practical advice in this chapter will equip you to navigate the scaling journey with confidence and success.

Online Gold Rush

Chapter 14
Overcoming Challenges and Pitfalls

Common obstacles faced by online entrepreneurs

Strategies for handling setbacks and challenges

Staying resilient and adaptable

In this chapter, we'll delve into the various challenges and pitfalls that online entrepreneurs frequently encounter as they embark on their journey to digital wealth. While the online business landscape offers abundant opportunities, it's essential to recognize and address the obstacles that may arise. We'll discuss common challenges, strategies for overcoming setbacks, and the critical importance of resilience and adaptability.

Common Obstacles Faced by Online Entrepreneurs

Starting and growing an online business can be rewarding, but it comes with its fair share of challenges. Let's explore these challenges in more depth and consider strategies for overcoming them:

Market Saturation:
Understanding Market Dynamics: Recognize that market saturation is a natural outcome of a competitive online landscape. For example, the smartphone market has become saturated with various brands and models.

Niche Identification: Identify niches or unique value propositions that can set your business apart. For instance, Dollar Shave Club identified a niche in affordable, subscription-based razors in a market dominated by expensive brands.

Continuous Innovation: Stay ahead by continually innovating your products, services, or content. Amazon is an excellent example of a company that consistently innovates and disrupts various markets.

Financial Constraints:
Effective Financial Management: Develop a comprehensive financial plan, as Shopify did early on, which included budgeting, cash flow management, and financial projections.

Funding Options: Explore various funding options, like Kickstarter or venture capital, similar to how Airbnb secured funding in its early stages.

Lean Startup Approach: Adopt a lean startup approach by focusing on essential activities and minimizing unnecessary expenditures, as Dropbox did before achieving widespread success.

Technology Hurdles:
Technical Expertise: Invest in developing technical expertise within your team or consider outsourcing technical tasks to experts when necessary. For example, Netflix built its own content delivery network to handle streaming technology.

Website Maintenance: Regularly maintain and update your website to ensure it functions smoothly and remains secure. WordPress is a content management system (CMS) that simplifies website management for many businesses.

Cybersecurity: Protect your online business and customer data from cyber threats, as Equifax had to do after a major data breach. Implement robust cybersecurity measures, including firewalls, encryption, and regular security audits.

Changing Algorithms:
Adaptive Strategies: Stay informed about algorithm updates and adapt your strategies accordingly, much like content creators on YouTube or Instagram who adapt to platform changes.

Diversification: Diversify your online presence across multiple platforms to reduce dependency on a single channel. For instance, businesses use both Google Ads and Facebook Ads to reach different audiences.

Data-Driven Decisions: Monitor your online metrics and use data to make informed decisions, similar to how Airbnb uses data to optimize its pricing and user experience.

Customer Acquisition:
Content Marketing: Create valuable, relevant, and engaging content to attract and retain customers, akin to HubSpot's inbound marketing strategy.

Social Media Engagement: Leverage social media platforms to engage with your audience, share content, and build a community, as exemplified by brands like Nike and their social media engagement.

Customer Loyalty Programs: Implement customer loyalty programs to retain existing customers and encourage repeat purchases, like the Starbucks Rewards program.

Strategies for Handling Setbacks and Challenges

Entrepreneurship is inherently challenging, and setbacks are part of the journey. Here's a detailed exploration of strategies for handling these obstacles effectively:

Resilience:
Growth Mindset: Cultivate a growth mindset, similar to how Elon Musk views failures as opportunities for learning and growth.

Seeking Support: Don't hesitate to seek support from friends, family, mentors, or support groups, as entrepreneurs like Richard Branson have done throughout their careers.

Positive Outlook: Maintain a positive outlook by focusing on solutions rather than dwelling on problems, which is a mindset shared by many successful entrepreneurs.

Problem-Solving:
Frameworks and Techniques: Familiarize yourself with problem-solving frameworks, like Toyota's "5 Whys" or Six Sigma's DMAIC, which many organizations use to address issues systematically.

Root Cause Analysis: Use root cause analysis techniques to identify the underlying causes of problems, as Toyota did when addressing quality issues in its manufacturing processes.

Brainstorming: Encourage brainstorming sessions with your team or mentors to generate creative solutions to challenges, similar to how Google fosters innovation.

Adaptability:
Embrace Change: Embrace change as a natural part of the entrepreneurial journey, as exemplified by companies like Apple, which has pivoted its product offerings multiple times.

Continuous Learning: Foster a culture of continuous learning within your organization, much like how Amazon continually seeks new opportunities and innovations.

Agility in Decision-Making: Develop the ability to make agile decisions in fast-changing environments, similar to how Tesla adapts its manufacturing processes.

Networking and Mentorship:
Peer Networks: Build a network of peers within your industry or entrepreneurial community, as many successful entrepreneurs do.

Mentorship: Seek out mentors who have experience in your field or have overcome similar challenges, like how Mark Zuckerberg sought guidance from Steve Jobs.

Online Communities: Join online forums, social media groups, or platforms designed for entrepreneurs to connect with like-minded individuals facing similar challenges.

Resourcefulness:
Efficient Resource Allocation: Develop the ability to allocate resources efficiently, similar to how companies like IKEA focus on cost-effective solutions.

Leveraging Existing Assets: Maximize the use of your existing assets, whether it's your team's skills, technology, or intellectual property, similar to how Google leverages its search technology in various products.

Collaboration: Consider partnerships or collaborations with other businesses or organizations that can provide additional resources or support in overcoming specific challenges.

Staying Resilient and Adaptable

Staying resilient and adaptable in the face of adversity is crucial for entrepreneurs. Here's a detailed exploration of strategies for maintaining resilience and adaptability:

Psychological Resilience:
Emotional Regulation: Develop emotional regulation skills to manage your reactions to challenges, as practiced by many successful entrepreneurs.

Stress Management: Implement effective stress management techniques, such as exercise or mindfulness, to reduce the impact of stress on your well-being.

Coping Mechanisms: Identify healthy coping mechanisms that work for you, much like how Warren Buffett uses humor as a coping mechanism.

Building a Support System:
Family and Friends: Lean on your personal network for emotional support, as Oprah Winfrey often emphasizes the importance of her support system.

Entrepreneurial Communities: Connect with fellow entrepreneurs who understand the unique challenges you face, whether locally or through online communities.

Mentorship: Consider having a mentor or coach who can provide guidance, offer solutions, and share their own experiences in overcoming challenges.

Learning from Setbacks:
Reflective Practice: Engage in reflective practice by analyzing the causes and consequences of setbacks, similar to how Thomas Edison famously learned from his numerous failed experiments.

Resilience Building: Understand that resilience is built through adversity, and each challenge you overcome makes you more resilient and better prepared for the future.

Strategic Planning: In your strategic planning process, consider potential challenges and risks that your business might encounter. This proactive approach allows you to develop contingency plans in advance.

Seeking Professional Help:
Business Coaching: Consider working with a business coach or consultant who specializes in helping entrepreneurs navigate challenges, much like Tony Robbins does for business leaders.

Therapeutic Support: For personal challenges that impact your resilience and adaptability, don't hesitate to seek professional therapeutic support, as many entrepreneurs have done.

Case Studies and Success Stories: Extracting Insights and Inspiration
Analyzing case studies and success stories of entrepreneurs who overcame significant challenges can provide valuable insights and inspiration for your entrepreneurial journey. Here's a detailed exploration of how to approach and extract lessons from such stories:

Selecting Relevant Case Studies:
*Identify case studies and success stories that closely align with your industry, business model, or the specific challenges you're currently facing. This relevance makes the insights more actionable.

Contextual Understanding: Start by gaining a deep understanding of the context of each case study. Explore the challenges, setbacks, and obstacles the entrepreneurs encountered. Pay attention to the industry landscape, market conditions, and any unique circumstances.

Key Challenges and Obstacles: Highlight the main challenges and obstacles faced by the entrepreneurs. Understand how these challenges threatened their businesses and what impact they had on their operations.

Strategies and Solutions: Analyze the strategies, solutions, and actions taken by the entrepreneurs to address the challenges. Identify innovative approaches, decisions, or pivots they made to navigate difficult situations.

Resilience and Adaptability: Examine how the entrepreneurs demonstrated resilience and adaptability throughout their journeys. Explore how they responded to setbacks, remained flexible in their strategies, and learned from their experiences.

Key Turning Points: Identify pivotal moments or turning points in the case studies. These moments often represent critical decisions or actions that significantly influenced the outcome.

Learning Lessons: Extract key lessons from each case study. Consider how the strategies employed by successful entrepreneurs can be applied to your own challenges or opportunities.

Inspiration and Motivation: Recognize the inspirational aspects of each success story. Understand the determination, perseverance, and vision that drove these entrepreneurs to overcome adversity. Use their stories as a source of motivation during challenging times.

Application to Your Journey: Translate the insights and lessons learned into actionable steps for your own entrepreneurial journey. Consider how you can adapt their strategies to your specific circumstances and goals.

Continuous Learning: Remember that case studies and success stories are just one source of learning. Stay committed to continuous learning by exploring a variety of resources, including books, podcasts, and networking opportunities.

Mentorship and Networking: If possible, connect with the entrepreneurs featured in the case studies or seek mentorship from experienced individuals who have faced similar challenges. Personal interactions can provide additional insights and guidance.

Document Your Journey: As you face challenges and implement strategies inspired by case studies, document your own journey. This documentation can serve as a valuable resource for your future growth and as a source of inspiration for others.

By the end of this chapter, you'll be well-equipped with the knowledge and strategies needed to tackle challenges and navigate pitfalls that may arise in your online entrepreneurial journey. Staying resilient, adaptable, and resourceful is key to achieving long-term success in the ever-evolving digital landscape.

Online Gold Rush

Chapter 15
Celebrating Success and Future Horizons

Recognizing your achievements

Setting new goals and objectives

Continuing to innovate and adapt in the ever-changing online landscape

Recognizing Your Achievements:

Celebrating Milestones in Your Entrepreneurial Journey

Recognizing and celebrating your achievements is a crucial aspect of maintaining motivation, fostering a positive mindset, and sustaining long-term success in your online entrepreneurship journey. Here are more detailed explanations and examples:

Reflecting on Milestones: Taking dedicated time to reflect on the milestones you've achieved is essential. For example, if you started as a freelance content writer, reflect on how you've progressed from landing your first client to building a thriving writing business.

Celebrating Wins, Big and Small: Celebrate both significant victories and small wins along the way. Suppose you run an e-commerce store. A significant victory might be reaching your first $10,000 in monthly revenue, while a small win could be receiving five-star reviews from satisfied customers.

Gratitude and Acknowledgment: Express gratitude for the support and contributions of those who played a role in your success. If you've received mentorship from an industry expert, acknowledge their guidance publicly and thank your team for their hard work.

Defining Success Metrics: Clearly define what success means to you and your business. For instance, if you run a subscription box service, success might mean achieving a certain percentage of customer retention over a year.

Measuring Success: Regularly assess and measure your progress against the success metrics you've defined. If you set a goal to increase website traffic by 20%, track your traffic growth and celebrate when you achieve that milestone.

Personal Growth and Development: Reflect on how you've grown as an entrepreneur and as an individual. For instance, if you're a tech startup founder, recognize how your leadership skills have evolved as you've navigated challenges.

Sharing Achievements: Share your achievements with your audience. If you're a fitness influencer, share your before-and-after photos, celebrating your fitness journey. These posts can inspire others and show your authenticity.

Setting New Goals: After celebrating an achievement, consider setting new, challenging goals. For example, if you're a podcast host, after reaching 10,000 downloads per episode, set a new goal to reach 50,000 downloads.

Maintaining a Positive Mindset: The act of recognizing achievements contributes to maintaining a positive mindset. If you're a software developer, acknowledging the successful launch of a new app can boost your confidence and motivation.

Regularly Reflecting: Make the process of recognizing achievements and setting new goals a regular part of your entrepreneurial routine. As a content creator, regularly evaluate your content performance and adjust your strategies.

Setting New Goals and Objectives for Your Online Business

Setting new goals and objectives is a fundamental part of maintaining progress and growth in your online business. Here's a more detailed exploration with examples:

Goal Setting: Define clear and actionable goals for your online business. If you're in e-commerce, set a SMART goal to increase online sales by 30% within the next six months.

SMART Goals: Utilize the SMART framework effectively. If you're a software-as-a-service (SaaS) company, set a specific goal to reduce customer churn rate by 15% (measurable) in the next quarter (time-bound).

Diversifying Ventures: Explore opportunities to diversify your online ventures. For instance, if you're a fashion blogger, consider diversifying by launching your own clothing line or collaborating with fashion brands.

Innovation: Innovation is crucial for staying relevant. If you operate a mobile app development company, continuously explore new technologies like augmented reality (AR) to enhance your app offerings.

Market Trends: Stay informed about industry trends. If you run a digital marketing agency, staying updated on emerging advertising platforms, such as TikTok, allows you to adapt your services accordingly.

Strategic Planning: Develop a strategic plan outlining how you intend to achieve your newly established goals. As a startup founder, create a roadmap detailing product development, marketing strategies, and sales targets.

Monitoring and Adaptation: Regularly monitor your progress toward these new goals. If you operate a subscription-based software company, monitor customer feedback and adapt your product based on user suggestions.

Aligning with Your Vision: Ensure that your new goals align with your long-term vision for your online business. If your vision is to provide eco-friendly products, set goals related to sustainability and ethical sourcing.

Accountability and Review: Assign responsibility for each goal. In an e-learning platform, designate team members responsible for increasing user engagement and review progress during weekly meetings.

Flexibility: While setting new goals is important, be flexible enough to adjust them if circumstances change. If you're a content creator, adapt your content calendar to cover trending topics or address current events.

Continuing to Innovate and Adapt in Your Online Business

Innovation and adaptability are critical for long-term success in the ever-changing online business landscape. Here's a more detailed exploration with examples:

Adapting to Change: Recognize that the online landscape is dynamic. If you run a social media agency, adapt your strategies to changes in algorithms and user behavior on platforms like Facebook and Instagram.

Encouraging Technology Adoption: Stay at the forefront of technology adoption. If you operate a cloud-based software company, regularly update your software to incorporate the latest security features and integrations.

Customer-Centric Approach: Prioritize a customer-centric approach. As an e-commerce store owner, actively seek feedback from customers to improve their shopping experience and product offerings.

Competitive Analysis: Regularly analyze your competition. If you're in the e-learning space, monitor competitors' course offerings and pricing to identify areas where you can differentiate and excel.

Networking and Collaboration: Actively engage with other professionals. If you're a freelance graphic designer, collaborate with web developers to offer comprehensive design and development services.

Continuous Learning: Encourage a culture of continuous learning. If you manage a remote team, invest in training programs to keep your employees updated on the latest industry best practices.

Innovation Culture: Foster an innovation culture. If you're a tech startup founder, create an environment where team members are encouraged to propose and experiment with new ideas.

Strategic Planning: Develop a strategic plan with contingencies for adapting to unforeseen changes. If you operate a digital marketing agency, outline backup strategies for campaigns that aren't delivering the expected results.

Feedback Loops: Establish feedback loops both internally and externally. If you manage a software development team, gather input from customers and developers to make informed decisions.

Resource Allocation: Allocate resources specifically for innovation initiatives. If you're in the fintech sector, allocate a portion of your budget to research and development for new financial products.

Case Studies and Insights: Learning from Successful Online Entrepreneurs

In this chapter, we delve into case studies of accomplished online entrepreneurs who have navigated challenges, celebrated their achievements, set new goals, and embraced innovation. Here's a more detailed look at how these case studies and insights can benefit you:

Learning from Diverse Experiences: Case studies encompass a range of online businesses. For example, if you're in the health and wellness industry, studying successful fitness apps, meal kit delivery services, and fitness influencers can provide diverse insights.

Identifying Common Patterns: Analyzing multiple case studies allows you to identify common patterns. If you're in the e-commerce sector, you may notice that successful brands consistently prioritize user experience and customer reviews.

Overcoming Challenges: Case studies often highlight the obstacles and setbacks entrepreneurs faced. If you're a software startup founder, learning how successful software companies overcame initial technical challenges can be invaluable.

Celebrating Achievements: Successful entrepreneurs often share their milestones and achievements. If you're a content creator, sharing your journey from your first 1,000 subscribers to your first sponsorship deal can inspire your audience.

Setting New Goals: Case studies often include stories of entrepreneurs who set ambitious goals. If you run a consulting firm, you can learn how successful consultants expanded their services and client base after achieving initial success.

Innovation and Adaptation: Many case studies showcase how entrepreneurs embraced innovation. For example, if you're in the travel industry, studying how travel startups pivoted during the COVID-19 pandemic can inform your own adaptation strategies.

Strategic Decision-Making: Successful entrepreneurs are often faced with critical decisions. If you're a tech startup founder, understanding the decision-making processes of successful startups can help you navigate similar choices.

Resourceful Problem-Solving: Entrepreneurs often find resourceful solutions to complex problems. If you operate an e-commerce business, learning how successful e-commerce entrepreneurs optimized their supply chains can improve your operations.

Networking and Collaboration: Some entrepreneurs attribute their success to strategic partnerships. If you run a marketing agency, studying how agencies collaborated with influencers or complementary service providers can inform your partnership strategies.

Continuous Learning: Successful entrepreneurs emphasize the importance of continuous learning. If you're in the education sector, following the journeys of educators who continuously updated their curriculum and teaching methods can inspire your own educational initiatives.

Inspiration and Motivation: Reading about the journeys of accomplished entrepreneurs can serve as a source of inspiration and motivation. Whether you're in the fashion industry or finance, these stories remind you that success is achievable with determination and the right strategies.

By the end of this book, you'll be well-equipped to not only build a profitable online business but also to celebrate your successes, set ambitious goals, and thrive in the dynamic digital landscape. Your journey toward digital wealth is an ongoing adventure, and with the right mindset and strategies, your potential for growth and innovation is limitless.

Final Words

As we conclude this enlightening journey through **"Online Gold Rush**: Navigating the Road to Digital Wealth," it's essential to reflect on the remarkable voyage we've undertaken together.

In the span of these chapters, we've delved deep into the dynamic realm of online entrepreneurship, armed with **ChatGPT** as our trusted ally. From the inception in Chapter 1, where we established the foundations of our online ambitions, to Chapter 15, where we set our sights on future horizons, the road has been one of discovery, learning, and transformation.

We've unveiled the wealth of opportunities that the digital world offers today, but equally important, we've discussed setting realistic expectations for your online endeavors. The significance of the right mindset and unwavering commitment has been emphasized, for it is these qualities that will propel you towards success.

Through the chapters that followed, we've harnessed the power of **ChatGPT**, understanding its capabilities and witnessing real-world examples of businesses thriving through its integration. We've honed in on the importance of identifying your niche, building a robust online presence, and crafting compelling content that resonates with your audience.

Monetization strategies, audience growth tactics, SEO mastery, and data-driven decision-making have all been unwrapped for you, with **ChatGPT** as a constant companion. In overcoming challenges and pitfalls, we've fostered resilience and adaptability, critical qualities in the digital landscape.

And now, as we reach the culmination of this journey, we encourage you to recognize your achievements, both small and significant. Set new goals, reach for higher horizons, and, above all, continue to innovate and adapt. The online world is ever-evolving, and your success lies in your ability to ride the waves of change.

"Online Gold Rush" has equipped you with the tools, knowledge, and strategies to make money online effectively within just six months. It has shown you that **ChatGPT** is not just a tool but a valuable ally in your pursuit of digital wealth.

As you turn the last page, remember that your journey has only just begun. The digital frontier is vast, and your potential is limitless. Go forth, navigate the road to digital wealth, and let your success be the testament to the power of determination, innovation, and **ChatGPT** as your guiding star.

Your adventure awaits. Start now and seize your place in the digital gold rush.